Teacher's Manual

Building English Skills

Blue Level
Revised Edition

Prepared by **Janet M. Gibson**

Patricia Hoepfner Meyer

Susan Duffy Schaffrath

McDougal, Littell & Company

Evanston, Illinois
Sacramento, California

ISBN: 0-88343-885-2

Contents

1 The Books in the BUILDING ENGLISH SKILLS Series

Red Level (Grade 7)

Composition

1 The Story of Our Language
2 Building Your Vocabulary
3 Using the Senses
4 Writing Paragraphs
5 Ways of Developing Paragraphs
6 Kinds of Paragraphs
7 Writing the Composition
8 Kinds of Compositions
9 Writing Letters
10 Using the Library
11 Developing Your Speaking and Listening Skills

Grammar, Usage, and Mechanics

1 The Sentence and Its Parts
2 Using Verbs
3 Using Nouns
4 Using Pronouns
5 Using Adjectives
6 Using Adverbs
7 Using Prepositions and Conjunctions
8 Compound Sentences
9 Making Subjects and Verbs Agree
10 Capitalization
11 Punctuation
12 Spelling

Green Level (Grade 8)

Composition

1 Developing Your Vocabulary
2 Using the Dictionary
3 Writing the Paragraph
4 Developing the Paragraph
5 Different Kinds of Paragraphs
6 Writing the Composition
7 Kinds of Compositions
8 Writing Social and Business Letters
9 Thinking Clearly
10 The Library and How To Use It
11 Interviews and Group Discussions

Grammar, Usage, and Mechanics

1 The Simple Sentence
2 Using Nouns
3 Using Pronouns
4 Using Verbs
5 Using Modifiers
6 Using Prepositions and Conjunctions
7 Using Compound and Complex Sentences
8 Making Subjects and Verbs Agree
9 Using Verbals
10 Capitalization
11 Punctuation
12 Spelling

Orange Level (Grade 9)

Composition

1 Building Your Vocabulary
2 Using the Senses in Writing
3 Improving Your Sentences
4 The Process of Writing
5 Writing Effective Paragraphs
6 Types of Paragraphs
7 Writing a Composition
8 Types of Compositions
9 Writing Letters
10 Using the Library
11 Giving a Talk

Grammar, Usage, and Mechanics

1 The Sentence and Its Parts
2 Using Complete Sentences
3 Using Nouns
4 Using Pronouns
5 Using Verbs
6 Using Modifiers
7 Using Prepositions and Conjunctions
8 Review of Parts of Speech
9 Using Verbals
10 Making Subjects and Verbs Agree
11 Using Compound and Complex Sentences
12 The Right Word
13 Capitalization
14 Punctuation
15 Spelling
16 The Correct Form for Writing

Blue Level (Grade 10)

Composition

1 Building Your Vocabulary
2 Using the Dictionary To Build Word Power
3 Combining Ideas in Sentences
4 Improving Your Sentences
5 The Process of Writing
6 Writing Effective Paragraphs
7 Developing the Paragraph
8 Writing a Composition or a Report
9 Types of Compositions
10 Letters, Applications, and Résumés
11 Using the Library and Reference Works
12 Group Discussion

Handbook

1 The Classification of Words
2 The Parts of a Sentence
3 Sentence and Clause
4 Complete Sentences
5 Agreement of Subject and Verb
6 Pronoun Usage
7 Adjective and Adverb Usage
8 Verb Usage
9 The Right Word
10 Capitalization
11 End Marks and Commas
12 The Semicolon, the Colon, the Dash, and Parentheses
13 The Apostrophe
14 Quotations
15 Spelling
16 The Plurals of Nouns
17 Good Manuscript Form
18 Outlining

Yellow Level (Grade 11)

Composition

1 Developing Your Vocabulary
2 Examining Word Parts
3 Writing Effective Sentences
4 Revising Your Sentences
5 Achieving Sentence Clarity
6 Achieving Sentence Variety
7 The Process of Writing
8 Writing the Paragraph
9 Ways of Developing the Paragraph
10 Writing a Composition
11 Writing the Paraphrase and the Summary
12 Writing a Research Report
13 Using Figurative Language
14 Clear Thinking
15 Using the Library and Reference Materials

Handbook

1 The Classification of Words
2 The Parts of a Sentence
3 Sentence and Clause
4 Complete Sentences
5 Agreement of Subject and Verb
6 Pronoun Usage
7 Adjective and Adverb Usage
8 Verb Usage
9 The Right Word
10 Capitalization
11 End Marks and Commas
12 The Semicolon, the Colon, the Dash, and Parentheses
13 The Apostrophe
14 Quotations
15 Spelling
16 The Plurals of Nouns
17 The Forms of Letters
18 Good Manuscript Form

Purple Level (Grade 12)

Composition

1 Vocabulary Development
2 Sentence Combining
3 Effective Sentences
4 Sentence Revision
5 Sentence Clarity
6 Sentence Variety
7 The Process of Writing
8 The Paragraph: Its Structure
9 The Paragraph: Its Other Elements
10 Types of Paragraphs
11 The Composition
12 The Paraphrase and the Summary
13 Writing About Literature
14 The Research Paper
15 The Library and Its Reference Materials

Handbook

1 The Classification of Words
2 The Parts of a Sentence
3 Sentence and Clause
4 Complete Sentences
5 Agreement of Subject and Verb
6 Pronoun Usage
7 Adjective and Adverb Usage
8 Verb Usage
9 The Right Word
10 Capitalization
11 End Marks and Commas
12 The Semicolon, the Colon, the Dash, and Parentheses
13 The Apostrophe
14 Quotations
15 Spelling
16 The Plurals of Nouns
17 The Forms of Letters
18 Good Manuscript Form

2   Special Features of the BUILDING ENGLISH SKILLS Series

The emphasis of the *Building English Skills* series is on the skills and art of communication through the use of language. To this end, the series focuses on three main areas necessary for effective communication:

1. Thinking
2. Writing
3. Speaking

The Vocabulary Chapters

Because effective communication must rely on words, vocabulary study is an important part of the *Building English Skills* series. Each book in the series begins with a chapter on vocabulary development.

The chapters are designed to engage students' interest in words—what they mean, how they are used, how they are formed. Building an effective vocabulary is a cumulative process and students are taught the skills by which they can gradually expand their vocabularies by themselves. A large vocabulary is the basis for the selection and refinement of the words that control effective communication.

The vocabulary chapters emphasize four constant principles in the study of words:

1. Most words have more than one meaning.
2. The meaning of a particular word depends upon the context in which it is used.
3. Both context and word parts provide clues to the meanings of unfamiliar words.
4. Many encounters with a word are necessary to determine its different meanings.

The Sentence Improvement Chapters

The *Building English Skills* series offers a program of sentence improvement based on the authors' analysis of over 3000 student themes. The sentence improvement program is rooted in the belief that *the important problems of writing begin at the level of the sentence.* Some of these problems involve errors in grammar, but many of them are problems of meaning and sense. In each book a chapter is devoted to those sentences which, though grammatically correct, are nonetheless unsatisfactory. Each book, for example, deals with *empty sentences,* the circular sentences that say nothing:

I have a minor crisis in my life, and to me it presents a problem.

Each book deals with *padded sentences* like the following:

What I mean is that his ideas of summer camp are not realistic.

Each book deals with *overloaded sentences*, the sentences that contain too many ideas:

In my frenzied rush to get to the patient's tray, I failed to notice the sign on the door and I walked in and I noticed the woman was very pale and suddenly I realized I was in an isolation room.

In *Building English Skills, Blue Level,* Chapter 4 deals with sentences such as those shown above. Such unsatisfactory sentences arise from clearly identifiable causes that can be isolated and presented in a non-grammatical analysis.

The Composition Chapters

The ability to communicate correctly and effectively in writing is becoming increasingly more important in today's world, whether in college or on the job. The *Building English Skills* series places a major emphasis on writing. The composition chapters are teaching chapters that enable the student to move step-by-step through the process of writing.

The writing process in an overall pattern moves through four steps in this series:

1. Deciding upon a topic

2. Organizing and developing the topic

3. Writing clearly and effectively

4. Revising and refining

In working through this process, students are given models of fine writing, along with helpful analysis. They are given help in finding content for their writing. They are taught how to organize and develop the different kinds of paragraphs that are appropriate for their purpose. They are aided in writing clearly and effectively, and they are taught how to revise and refine.

The Handbook of Grammar and Usage

The second half of each book in the series consists of a Handbook. This Handbook contains a comprehensive statement of grammar, usage, capitalization, punctuation, spelling, and manuscript form.

Distinctive Features of the Handbook. The Handbook has some distinct advantages over other available handbooks:

1. The typographic arrangement is clear and attractive. Type and open space have been used to set off usages, examples, and definitions so as to make them easy to find and easy to read.
2. Since each topic is a short phrase (printed in red) rather than a rule, it is easy to locate.
3. Within each topic, there is a full explanation of each concept, followed by examples and, where appropriate, by the definition or generalization printed in boldface type.
4. Numerous exercises are provided for practice and reinforcement.

The Handbook for each grade level is a full *teaching* handbook. The explanations of forms and usages and the exercise material have been carefully adapted to meet the needs of each grade level.

Related Materials

Skills Practice Books. For each grade level the series includes a soft-cover consumable workbook with additional skill-building exercises. Each perforated page (front and back) constitutes a self-contained teaching unit, complete with an introductory lesson and dozens of exercises. This convenient feature makes these books easy for teachers to use and ideal for independent skills practice.

Diagnostic and Mastery Tests. A separate booklet of diagnostic and mastery tests is also available for each level. The diagnostic tests identify problem areas in grammar, usage, capitalization, punctuation, and spelling. The mastery tests provide an overall "final examination" on those topics, while serving the additional function of reinforcing the various skills.

Duplicating Masters. The pages in the *Skills Practice Books* are also available in the form of Duplicating Masters.

3   The Content of BUILDING ENGLISH SKILLS Blue Level

The Composition Chapters (First half of the text)

Vocabulary Development. Chapter 1 emphasizes the study of *prefixes*, *suffixes*, and *roots and word families.* Chaper 2 analyzes each item of a dictionary entry as a basis for building word power. An adequate vocabulary, and the ability to use synonyms precisely, are prerequisites to good writing.

Sentence Combining. Chapter 3 presents a basic course in sentence combining. Its purpose is to help students create mature sentences, and to help them become aware of the options open to them in combining ideas.

Sentence Improvement. Chapter 4 provides an intensive program for sentence improvement based on a study of over 3000 student themes. The chapter is devoted to those sentences which, though grammatically correct, are nonetheless unsatisfactory. It deals with empty sentences, the circular sentences that say nothing; it also deals with overloaded sentences, the sentences that contain too many ideas.

The Process of Writing. Chapter 5 analyzes the three major steps in writing: *pre-writing*; *writing the first draft*; and *rewriting, or revising*, which includes proofreading.

The Paragraph. Chapters 6 and 7 comprise an intensive study of the paragraph. Chapter 6 emphasizes unity and coherence, and the importance of the topic sentence. Chapter 7 treats in detail the narrative paragraph, the descriptive paragraph, and the explanatory paragraph. Both chapters provide a wealth of first-rate models, along with helpful analysis.

The Composition. Chapter 8 provides a clear, workable blueprint for an expository composition, or report. Chapter 9 deals with narrative, descriptive, and explanatory compositions.

Letters, Applications, and Résumés. Chapter 10 presents the proper forms for business letters and discusses various types of business letters. It also provides help in filling out college and job applications and in writing résumés.

The Library and Reference Works. Chapter 11 provides an important means of helping students find subjects and source material for their writing.

Group Discussion. Chapter 12 helps students participate effectively in group discussion.

The Handbook (Second half of the text)

The Handbook is arranged in 18 numbered sections, as follows:

Grammar. Sections 1-4 provide a thorough treatment of grammar in a contemporary setting.

Usage. Sections 5-9 deal with problems of usage.

Capitalization, Punctuation, Spelling, and Manuscript Form. Sections 10-18 deal with the mechanics of writing.

Each Handbook Section is followed by a Review of the material covered in that section.

4   A Suggested Course of Study

Building English Skills, Blue Level is designed as a thorough, detailed course of study for tenth-grade students. The chapters are developed logically and sequentially so that the teacher need not construct a new order of presentation as is necessary with some texts. The chapters are arranged with word study preceding the writing of sentences; the writing of sentences preceding the writing of paragraphs; the writing of paragraphs preceding the writing of longer compositions; and so on.

The learning and reviewing of aspects of grammar and usage should be interposed whenever the students need it. The Handbook, which contains a complete presentation of grammar, usage, capitalization, punctuation, and spelling, should be referred to as often as the teacher feels necessary. If results of the Diagnostic Tests reveal the need to reteach certain aspects of grammar or usage, the teacher may set aside some time during the year for that purpose.

The text is arranged as a course of study for a broad range of tenth-grade students. Specific suggestions for meeting the needs of advanced students and less-advanced students are included throughout the Teacher's Manual.

5 Teaching Suggestions for
BUILDING ENGLISH SKILLS
Blue Level

Chapter 1

Building Your Vocabulary Pages 1–15

Objectives

1. To review frequently used prefixes and suffixes

2. To recognize common Latin roots

3. To become conscious of word parts as an aid to unlocking the meanings of unfamiliar words

Introduction

Aristophanes said it well: "By the words the mind is excited and the spirit elated." This chapter aims to extend the students' knowlege of words and word parts, specifically of prefixes, suffixes, and roots. The concepts presented will help the students build more fluent, forceful vocabularies. In a way, this chapter serves as the basis for the chapters that follow, for without a resourceful vocabulary, a student most assuredly will have difficulty in communicating orally and in writing.

Teaching Techniques. Following are suggestions for teaching vocabulary in a classroom setting.

1. **Vocabulary Quizzes.** Each week, give the students a maximum of ten words. Three of these words should have the same prefix, suffix, or root. Require the students to learn the spelling, part of speech, definition, and a synonym (if applicable) for each word, and to use it in a sentence. You might also ask them to illustrate the meaning of at least one word; for example, if the word *manacle* were on the list for a particular week, a student could draw a criminal in handcuffs.

After the first quiz, the remainder of the quizzes should include a few words from previous weeks. At the end of a quarter, give a vocabulary exam covering all of the words given during that quarter. Begin the next quarter fresh, so as not to overwhelm the students with too many new words.

2. Reading. Students learn a great many words through reading. Do not hesitate to discuss unfamiliar words when they are encountered in classroom materials.

3. Spelling Bees. If used sparingly, spelling bees can be an effective review of vocabulary words. You might want to separate the students into two teams, which can challenge each other by asking for the spellings, synonyms, antonyms, sentences, and definitions of vocabulary words.

4. Vocabulary Journal. Instruct the students to keep a notebook in which they can record the etymology, definition, synonym, antonym, and derivation of each new word. They might also add newspaper or magazine article clippings that show the word in context.

5. Teacher Encouragement and Enthusiasm. Your use of interesting words and encouragement of a broadened vocabulary will help the students be successful with vocabulary work. Look for opportunities to give positive reinforcement to students who use precise, vivid vocabulary in class discussions and in written work.

ONE WORD OF CAUTION: Do not encourage the development of vocabulary for its own sake. All words should be useful to the student.

Part 1

Prefixes

Pages 2–5

Review the definition of *prefix* with the class and the two types of prefixes: those having a single meaning and those having two or more meanings. Ask the students for additional examples of words that begin with each prefix.

Exercises. Exercises A–D on pages 4 and 5 can be completed as a class activity, by groups of four or five students working together, or individually by the students as a homework assignment. Remind the class to refer to the information on pages 2 and 3 as necessary. (See Keys to Exercises.)

Less-Advanced Students. Encourage these students to consult the dictionary for help in completing Exercises A, B, and D.

Advanced Students. Have these students page through a dictionary to compile a list of supplementary examples for each prefix.

Part 2
Suffixes
Pages 5–9

As you begin this section, clarify the meaning of *suffix*. Explain that there are two basic types of suffixes—noun suffixes and adjective suffixes—and that they are treated separately in this section.

Noun Suffixes. Remind the students that suffixes can help them identify the parts of speech. Review the noun suffixes on page 6, having the students suggest additional words that end in each suffix.

Exercises. For Exercises A and B on page 7, refer the students to dictionaries to check the spellings of words. (See Keys to Exercises.)

Adjective Suffixes. The three most common types of adjective suffixes are listed on pages 7 and 8. Ask the students to contribute additional examples of words that end in each suffix. Discuss the meanings of these words to reinforce the meanings of the suffixes given in the text.

Exercises. Exercise A on page 9 could be handled orally. Refer the students to dictionaries to check responses. Exercises B and C should be assigned as individual work, then discussed in class. The words in Exercise D could be defined in groups or by students working in pairs. However, each student should be required to write an original sentence for each word. (See Keys to Exercises.)

Less-Advanced Students. Refer those students who have difficulty with spelling to a spelling dictionary, which presents numerous forms of each word.

Advanced Students. Challenge these students by having them each write ten difficult words that have suffixes and prefixes studied in this section. Have the students exchange papers and try to decipher the meanings of each other's words.

Part 3
Roots and Word Families
Pages 10–15

You might introduce this section with a brief explanation of how Latin roots became part of the English language. Using a map, locate Rome and the areas conquered by the Roman armies. Explain that words derived from Latin entered English directly, when Rome conquered Britain, and indirectly through other languages; for example the Anglo-Saxon conquerors of England introduced words that had been borrowed originally from Latin. Explain also that for hundreds of years Latin was the language of scholars and clergy, and common people adapted words from the vocabulary of the learned.

Exercises. Exercise A presents additional examples of words with the roots listed on page 10. Exercise B also requires use of this list. Be sure that all students can complete these exercises without difficulty before proceeding with the lesson. (See Keys to Exercises.)

Eight More Useful Latin Roots. Discuss this list before assigning Exercises A and B.

Exercises. Work individually or in a small group with those students who have difficulty with the exercises on pages 12 and 13. (See Keys to Exercises.)

Word Families. This is an important section, for if students are unable to identify a word in context, they must rely on dissecting the word itself. Knowledge of word families will save students time and will help them extend their vocabularies. It will also help them with standardized tests, such as the sophomore tests and college entrance exams.

Exercises. The exercises on pages 14 and 15 may be relatively easy for some students and quite difficult for others. Encourage the students who are having trouble to consult dictionaries to learn the meanings and roots of words. (See Keys to Exercises.)

Less-Advanced Students. These students may need individual help in completing the exercises. Those students who experience extreme difficulty with Exercises A and B should not be assigned Exercise C.

Advanced Students. Challenge these students to dissect the word *antidisestablishmentarianism* just for fun.

Chapter 2

Using the Dictionary To Build Word Power

Pages 17–31

Objectives

1. To interpret the information contained in a dictionary entry

2. To develop awareness of the multiple meanings of words

3. To refine vocabulary through the correct use of synonyms and antonyms

4. To explore interesting word origins

Introduction

This chapter explains in detail the kinds of information a dictionary has to offer. Throughout the lessons, emphasize the value of the dictionary as a practical resource for reading and writing. (If your class is using a particular set of dictionaries, you may be able to get additional material for teaching from the publisher of the dictionary.)

Part 1

Finding Information in the Dictionary

Pages 18–23

What's on a Dictionary Page? Students should refer to the dictionary page reproduced on pages 22 and 23 while you read the descriptions of *guide words*, *entry*, and *key*.

What's in a Dictionary Entry? Refer the students to the entry for the word *enmity* on page 22 as you read the description of the parts of an entry.

Entry word. Emphasize the practical value of being able to find the syllabication of a word in a dictionary.

Pronunciation. Emphasize that students need to become familiar with the pronunciation symbols used by the particular dictionary they are using. Point out that the key on page 23 shows the pronunciation symbols used by one dictionary, *Webster's New World Dictionary* (Students Edition). Mention that some words have more than one acceptable pronunciation.

Part of speech. Students should be familiar with the parts of speech, but if necessary, a quick review can be conducted.

Etymology. Devote a few minutes to an explanation of how words come into a language. (They are borrowed from other languages; new words are coined; acronyms become familiar words, proper nouns become common nouns). Note that Part 4 of this chapter focuses on interesting word origins.

Definition. Students' two most frequent reasons for looking up a word are (1) to learn its meaning and (2) to learn its spelling. Encourage the students to evaluate the definition of a word to be sure that it expresses precisely the idea that they want to convey.

Synonymy. Synonymies are especially helpful when students wish to avoid using the same word too many times in their writing. They also help students distinguish slight variations in the meanings of words.

Derived words. Point out how closely related the derived words are to the entry word. Have the students find on the sample dictionary page (pages 22 and 23) derived words with noun suffixes taught in Chapter 1, Part 2 (for example, *-er*, *-ship*, *-ment*).

Cross Reference. Guide the students in finding additional cross references on the sample dictionary page (in the entries for *enormity, ensign, entail,* and *ennui*).

Exercise. Have the students complete the exercise on page 21 independently. Follow with group discussion and individual help for those students who gave incorrect answers for more than two questions. (See Keys to Exercises.)

Less-Advanced Students. Direct these students to concentrate on the definitions and synonyms in dictionary entries.

Advanced Students. Expect these students to be able to interpret all the information contained in each dictionary entry. Provide guidance as necessary.

Part 2

The Multiple Meanings of Words

Pages 24–26

A good way to increase vocabulary is to learn additional meanings for known words. Open the discussion of this section by asking the students for examples of familiar words that have more than one meaning.

Exercises. Introduce Exercise A on page 25 by writing on the chalkboard a sentence for the first meaning of *front*. Ask volunteers to contribute sentences for the other meanings of *front*.

Assign Exercises B, C, and D as independent work to be completed with the help of a dictionary. After discussing these three exercises, assign Exercise E to be completed and turned in for evaluation. (See Keys to Exercises.)

Less-Advanced Students. Encourage these students to use the dictionary when they are reading and writing to check the meanings and spellings of words.

Advanced Students. Have these students use the dictionary to find five common words that have more than ten meanings and to use each word in five sentences to illustrate five different meanings.

Part 3

Refining Your Vocabulary

Pages 26–30

This part of the chapter is designed to help each student refine or sharpen vocabulary through the correct use of synonyms and antonyms.

Synonyms. It is suggested that you make available one or more dictionaries of synonyms (such as *Roget's Thesuarus*) for student use.

Exercises. Exercises A and B on page 28 should be discussed in class after the students have completed the assignment independently. Check the students' papers carefully to make sure they have used each synonym in a sentence that illustrates its specific meaning. Exercise C may be reserved for the more advanced students.

Antonyms. To reinforce the definition of *antonym*, ask the students for examples of words that are either exact or close opposites.

Exercises. Complete Exercise A on page 29 as a class activity. For Exercise B, allow the students to consult the dictionary as they work independently. (See Keys to Exercises.) The completed sentences for Exercise C should be turned in for evaluation.

Less-Advanced Students. These students may need extra help in using synonyms and antonyms in sentences. Remember to encourage them as often as possible so that they sustain interest in building their vocabularies.

Advanced Students. After these students have completed the exercises, have them compare and contrast several inanimate and animate objects, using as many synonyms and antonyms as possible. This exercise could be completed in the students' journals.

Part 4

Interesting Word Origins

Pages 30–31

The history of language is a fascinating subject, and many students will find this section especially interesting.

Exercises. Exercises A and B on pages 30 and 31 can be done quite easily by advanced students. Average students, however, may need some help in locating the necessary information in their dictionaries. After the students have completed the exercises, discuss the origin of each word.

Words Derived from People's Names. The students might enjoy making up additional examples of malapropisms.

Exercise. The exercise on page 31 can be assigned as independent work. Again, advanced students will have no problem completing the exercise; other students may need individual or small-group help in locating relevant information. (See Keys to Exercises.)

Less-Advanced Students. Part 4 might be omitted if these students are having difficulty in completing the preceding part of the chapter. You must decide whether a study of word origins will distract from the main goal of having the students look upon the dictionary as a practical aid to speaking and writing.

Advanced Students. Introduce these students to specialized dictionaries of etymology, borrowed from the school or local library.

Chapter 3

Combining Ideas in Sentences

Pages 33–47

Objectives

1. To join sentences that express similar ideas

2. To join related sentence parts

3. To combine sentences by adding ideas from one sentence to another

4. To combine sentences to show how ideas are related

5. To combine sentences to eliminate repetitiveness from groups of sentences

6. To combine sentences to eliminate choppiness

Introduction

Introduce this chapter by reading aloud the choppy set of sentences on page 33 and the combined version on page 34. Have the students read them and then suggest ways in which the two expressions of similar ideas are different. The students are likely to see that the combined version uses fewer words to say much the same thing, avoids some repetition, and sounds like the work of a better writer. If they do not notice it, point out that the combined version clearly states the reason for stopping at the diner, while the choppy version requires the reader to infer the reason. Explain that one mark of a good writer is the ability to find more than one way to express an idea and then to choose the best of several ways. Demonstrate this idea with the following versions of the combined sentence.

We stopped at an all-night diner after the game and had hamburgers and clam chowder, because we were all hungry.

At an all-night diner where we stopped because we were all hungry after the game, we had hamburgers and clam chowder.

Ask the students to suggest still other versions of the sentence, and then have them discuss the strengths and weaknesses of each. Explain that this chapter will help them achieve a similar flexibility and power in their own writing.

As the students work with the methods of sentence combining taught in this chapter, emphasize the meanings of the sentences involved, and not their grammatical structure. It is not necessary to avoid grammatical terminology entirely; however, the students will be better able to concentrate on the meanings of the sentences they write if they do not have to make a conscious effort to identify their grammatical structures.

Part 1

Joining Sentences

Pages 34–35

This section focuses simply on joining sentences with similar ideas. This skill is one of the earliest that a speaker of English learns, and the students should have little difficulty mastering it in writing. It serves as an introduction to sentence-combining techniques and as the basis for later learning. When discussing the examples on page 34, emphasize the fact that the choice of *and, but,* or *or* to join the sentences has a critical effect on the meaning.

Exercises. Assign and correct Exercise A on page 35 before assigning Exercise B. Since these are the students' first efforts at combining, have the students try a few of the sentences orally in class before they complete the exercise on their own. (See Keys to Exercises.)

Less-Advanced Students. These students may need help in identifying the relationships expressed by the sentences in Exercise B. Have them read the sentences aloud, discuss how they are related, and then try oral combinations before writing their answers.

Advanced Students. These students should complete Exercise A with ease and have little, if any, trouble with Exercise B. Caution them to guard against carelessness.

Part 2

Joining Sentence Parts

Pages 36–37

When discussing the examples on page 36, point out that the italicized words are repeated. Explain that *and*, *but*, or *or* joins the related ideas and eliminates the repetition. Have students explain how the ideas in each pair of example sentences are related. Stress the idea that only sentence parts that express related ideas of equal importance should be joined by *and*, *but*, or *or*.

Exercises. When assigning Exercise A, remind students that the italicized words are to be eliminated. When assigning Exercise B, point out that students will have to decide on their own which words to eliminate. (See Keys to Exercises.)

Less-Advanced Students. When checking Exercise A, identify those students who are having difficulty combining sentences. Work with them in a small group until they can join sentences according to the pattern taught in this Part. When assigning Exercise B, have students identify orally the repeated words in each pair of sentences. Suggest that the students write the sentences on scrap paper and cross out the repeated words before writing the combined sentences.

Advanced Students. Have the students decide whether any of the sentences in Exercise B might be combined in more than one way, using a different connecting word in each combination. Then have them explain the differences in meaning that result.

Part 3

Adding Single Words

Pages 37–38

Point out to the students that each of the words added in the examples on pages 37 and 38 describes a word in the first sentence. Be sure that they notice that the italicized words are to be eliminated even though they are not repeated words. Help students see how little meaning these words add to the uncombined sentences. Have students explain what changes of form occurred in the added words in the last two examples.

Exercises. Complete Exercise A as a class activity. Ask volunteers to write the revised sentences on the chalkboard and to circle the word that has been added to each. Assign Exercise B as independent work. Remind students that some words will be eliminated and that it may be necessary to change the form of a word before adding it to a sentence. (See Keys to Exercises.)

Less-Advanced Students. Have students suggest combinings for Exercise B orally before writing out their answers independently. Provide individual or small-group help for those students who have difficulty completing Exercise B.

Advanced Students. Have students search their own writing—perhaps their journals or previous writing assignments—for sentences that could be combined by using the techniques they have learned.

Part 4

Adding Several Single Words

Pages 39–40

When discussing the examples and explanatory material on page 39, emphasize that the main idea of a group of sentences should not be changed when they are combined. Have students explain how each of the details is related to the main idea in the example sentences.

Exercises. Complete the first two or three items in Exercise A with the class, and then assign the remainder of the exercise as independent work. When correcting the exercise, ask volunteers to write the revised sentences on the chalkboard and to circle the words that were incorporated from other sentences. Repeat the same procedure for Exercise B. (See Keys to Exercises.)

Less-Advanced Students. These students may need help deciding what words to eliminate in Exercise B and what changes of form the remaining words may need. Either pair them with advanced students or work with a small group to produce combinations orally before the students write their answers. Urge the students to use scrap paper when they work alone, so that they can try several combinations before writing their final answers.

Advanced Students. Challenge these students by asking them to add an original detail to each of the combined sentences they wrote for Exercise B.

Part 5

Adding Words with -ly

Page 41

When discussing the examples and explanatory material, again emphasize that the main idea of a group of sentences should not be changed when they are combined. Have students explain how each of the details is related to the main idea in the example sentences. Have students describe the changes in form that occurred in each of the added words.

Exercise. Assign and check the exercise in class. Work with any students who have difficulty, although all students are likely to be able to complete the exercise easily. (See Keys to Exercises.)

Part 6

Adding Groups of Words

Pages 41–43

Point out that the added group of words in each example describes a word in the first sentence. Emphasize that the words should be placed as close as possible to the word they describe. Illustrate the confusion that can result if they are misplaced. Write the following sentence on the chalkboard and have the students explain how its meaning differs from the corresponding example sentence on page 41.

A box stood in the corner filled with old clothes.

In contrast, point out the variety possible when a group of words describes or explains the entire main idea of a sentence. Explain that this is the kind of flexibility an accomplished writer enjoys.

Exercises. When assigning Exercise A, remind students to place the group of words as close as possible to the word they describe. After checking Exercise A, assign Exercise B. Mention that more than one combination is possible and "right" for some of the groups of sentences. The students should try to decide which is best for the meaning intended. (See Keys to Exercises.)

Less-Advanced Students. These students may have difficulty with the exercises because they involve four slightly different patterns for combining sentences. Have them explain orally what each detail describes. Then have them combine the sentences one at a time, speaking or writing the result of each combination, until all the details have been added to the first sentence.

Advanced Students. Encourage the students to write more than one version of any sentence for which more than one version makes sense. Have them compare the versions they have written and discuss how they differ.

Part 7

Combining with *-ing*

Pages 44–47

The combinings in this part require the greatest changes in form. The idea expressed by an entire sentence is inserted into another sentence. Students will be helped to understand the steps involved if the combining is performed on the chalkboard. First write the sentences to be combined. For example:

We stacked the cartons neatly. That helped us get more into the van.

Then show the change in form. For example, cross out *We stacked* and write above it *Stacking*. Next, erase the unnecessary word *that*, leaving the combined result.

Stacking the carton neatly helped us get more into the van.

Exercises. Have the students complete Exercise A as a class activity. If necessary, work out several of the combinings on the chalkboard. Then assign Exercise B as independent work. (See Keys to Exercises.)

Less-Advanced Students. Work with these students in a small group to produce combinations orally before having them write their combinations.

Advanced Students. Have these students help classmates who find Exercise B difficult.

Review Exercises

Less-Advanced Students. Select several items from each exercise rather than assigning the entire exercises. (See Keys to Exercises.)

Advanced Students. Increase the challenge for these students by selecting items from the review exercises to include on an exercise sheet without combining clues or general directions. Scramble the order of the items selected. Urge students to try a variety of ways of combining the ideas.

Chapter 4

Improving Your Sentences Pages 49–75

Objectives

1. To analyze and revise the following types of faulty sentences:

   Empty Sentences—sentences that are lacking in ideas, in substance
   Padded Sentences—sentences that are stretched out with unnecessary words
   Overloaded sentences—sentences that try to say too much

2. To understand the importance of omitting irrelevant details

3. To write sentences in which related sentence parts are kept together

4. To combine and subordinate ideas correctly

5. To become aware of the need for parallel structure

6. To realize the importance of revision as a normal part of the writing process

Introduction

This chapter explains eight ways to make sentences clear, concise and readable
1. Avoiding empty sentences
2. Avoiding padded sentences
3. Avoiding overloaded sentences
4. Keeping to the point
5. Keeping related sentence parts together
6. Combining ideas effectively
7. Subordinating ideas correctly
8. Making sentences parts parallel
The purpose of the lessons is to increase students' ability to recognize and revise common writing problems and to apply these skills to the revision of their own writing.

Part 1

Avoiding Empty Sentences

Pages 50–52

Direct the class's attention to the two sample sentences on page 50. Have the students compare the sentences and explain why the second sentence is more effective. From this discussion should emerge an awareness on the part of all students that a sentence can be grammatically correct and yet fail to communicate. Emphasize that *the function of the sentence is to convey one or more facts or ideas.*

Exercises. The ten sentences in Exercise A on page 51 give students a chance to revise empty sentences individually and then share their revisions with their classmates. The group should decide which revisions are best and for what reasons. Exercise B could be done in the same manner. Remind the students to use the three suggestions given in Exercise A for the completion of the second exercise. Stress that there is no single correct way to revise the exercise sentences. (See Key to Exercises.)

Less-Advanced Students. Some of these students may see nothing wrong with the empty sentences in the exercises. Work closely with these students, helping them to recognize the lack of substance in each sentence.

Advanced Students. The revisions done by these students will show a considerable amount of variety. After they have finished revising the sentences, they might share their revisions with each other and decide which ones are the most effective.

Part 2

Avoiding Padded Sentences

Pages 52–55

Many students are probably familiar with the term padded sentence. These kinds of sentences result from three basic faults:

a. **Repetition of the Same Word or Idea.** Additional examples of unnecessary repetitions include *a distance of ten yards, advance forward, an actual fact, free gift,* and *retreat back.* Ask the students to suggest other examples.

b. **Repetition of *That*.** The word *that* is often used too frequently. Read aloud the two padded sentences on page 53 so that the students can hear the unnecessary repetitions.

c. **The Use of Fillers.** Sentences containing fillers are sometimes difficult to revise because students cannot think of other ways to express the same ideas. The solution is to write new sentences with new beginnings and sometimes with new subject-verb combinations. Emphasize that it is usually best to express an idea in as few words as possible.

Exercises. Exercise A on pages 54 and 55 may be completed as oral class activity. Exercise B should be a written exercise, with discussion following. (See Keys to Exercises.)

Less-Advanced Students. The oral completion of Exercise A should help these students understand what is being done to the sentences.

Advanced Students. Expect quality work from these students, in the revision exercises in this chapter and in all other written work as well.

Part 3
Avoiding Overloaded Sentences
Pages 55–59

Explain the definition of an overloaded sentence; then direct students to the five steps on page 56 that will help them avoid such sentences. In earlier years, students learned that overloaded sentences are often caused by the use of too many connecting words (*and, so,* etc.) They now will learn, through study of the examples on pages 56 and 57, that many sentences can be revised effectively only by means of a major rethinking of the ideas to be conveyed, and a consequent restructuring of the sentences .

Exercises. Exercise A on page 58 may be handled effectively in groups of three or four students. Remind the class to refer to the three suggestions at the beginning of this exercise when revising the sentences. Exercise B should be completed independently. Exercise C on page 59 includes empty, padded, and overloaded sentences. This exercise could be a graded check of the concepts presented thus far in the chapter. (See Key to Exercises.)

Less-Advanced Students. While these students probably will not have difficulty separating overly long sentences, they may have problems rewording and condensing sentences. Individual assistance from you or selected advanced students might alleviate some of the problems.

Advanced Students. Even though these students might revise quite well, they might not rework their revisions. Encourage several revisions of each exercise sentence so that the students will do a superior rather than just an adequate job.

Part 4
Keeping to the Point
Pages 59–61

You should have no trouble explaining the kind of sentence problem introduced here. You might want to supplement the example on page 59 with sentences taken from the students' own writing or made up by advanced students.

Exercises. The sentences in Exercise A on page 60 should be read aloud in class to help the students recognize errors. Exercise B on page 61 should be assigned as written work. Advise students to read the directions several times before beginning the exercise. (See Key to Exercises.)

Less-Advanced Students. These students should have no problem in identifying irrelevant details in sentences; however, they might have difficulty analyzing and revising sentences with more than one error. The students' questions will guide you in providing specific help.

Advanced Students. Encourage these students to experiment with different ways of solving the sentence problems in Exercise B.

Part 5
Keeping Related Sentence Parts Together
Pages 61–63

Present the class with the following rules for constructing well written sentences: (1) keep the parts of a verb phrase together; (2) keep subject and verb as close together as possible; and (3) keep verb and object as close together as possible. The three examples on pages 61 and 62 illustrate the application of these rules in the revision process.

Exercises. Exercise A on pages 62 and 63 should be completed only after the suggestions have been read and reread by all students. You might want to revise the first sentence for the students before assigning the remainder of the sentences as independent work. Discussion should follow, and the various revisions should be shared and evaluated by the class. Exercise B on page 63 may serve as a graded exercise for the students. (See Key to Exercises.)

Less-Advanced Students. These students may have difficulty identifying subject and verb, the parts of a verb phrase, and the object of a verb. Explain to them that commas separating parts of a sentence generally indicate that those parts are out of place.

Advanced Students. This section should not be difficult for these students. Remind them that they should watch for errors like these in their future writing.

Part 6
Combining Ideas Effectively
Pages 63–67

Have a student read aloud the example of the string-of-ideas sentence on page 64. Emphasize the "three R's" of writing: reread, revise, and rewrite.

Using Compound Sentences Correctly. Guide the students in studying the examples on page 64. Point out that writers often assume that readers understand what they are saying, when in reality the readers are confused. Emphasize that the ideas in a compound sentence must be closely related.

Using Linking Words Correctly. Emphasize that linking words establish relationships between ideas. Note that a semicolon appears *before* a linking word and a comma *after* it.

Exercises. The six suggestions should be read by all students. You may then want to analyze the first sentence in Exercise A for the students before assigning the remainder of the sentences as independent work. Repeat the same procedure for Exercise B. Discuss thoroughly the relationships between the ideas in each sentence. (See Key to Exercises.)

Less-Advanced Students. You might suggest that these students consult Handbook Section 3.2 (The Compound Sentence).

Advanced Students. Prior to their next written assignment, encourage these students to combine ideas in sentences in a variety of ways.

Part 7
Subordinating Ideas Correctly
Pages 68–71

This section may be the most difficult in the chapter for even the advanced students. Begin the discussion by defining the difference between a subordinate clause and a main clause. You might want to refer the class to Handbook Section 1.7 (The Conjunction) and Section 3.3 (The Clause).

Problems in Joining Ideas. The first problem is faulty coordination. A careful reading of the explanation on page 68 and a study of the examples on pages 68 and 69 will clarify the problem and provide guidelines for revision that can be applied by most students.

The second problem is faulty subordination. Often less-advanced students who are guilty of faulty coordination have no problems with faulty subordination because their sentences are still primer-style. If possible, supplement the examples on pages 69 and 70 with examples taken from students' papers.

Exercises. Exercise A on page 70 deals only with faulty coordination. Exercise B, which deals with faulty subordination, may be very difficult for the less-advanced students and challenging for the advanced students. You may decide to review the students' work after they have revised two or three sentences. (See Key to Exercises.)

Less-Advanced Students. The terms *coordinating* and *subordinating* may confuse these students. You may want to substitute *main idea* and *less important idea*.

Advanced Students. If these students still have problems after doing the exercises or if you note continuing problems in the students' writing, do more work on subordinating ideas, using the Handbook lessons on the conjunction, the clause, and the complex sentence.

Part 8
Making Sentence Parts Parallel
Pages 71–75

Before discussing the examples on pages 71 and 72, write on the chalkboard the following sentences, which demonstrate the concept of parallelism: *He went to Paris, London, and Rome. He went to Paris, London, and to Rome. He went to Paris, London, and visited Rome. He went to Paris, to London, and to Rome.* Guide the class in identifying examples one and four as parallel in structure and examples two and three as not parallel.

Exercises. Complete Exercise A on page 73 as a class activity. Emphasize that there is not necessarily one correct way to reword each sentence. Exercise B on pages 73 and 74 might be a written exercise; the revisions can be discussed after the students have finished. (See Key to Exercises.)

Less-Advanced Students. These students will understand parallelism after they practice with many examples. You might ask the advanced students to write additional examples.

Advanced Students. Caution these students to watch for lack of parallelism in their own writing.

Review Exercises. Both Exercises A and B on pages 74 and 75 could be used to test the concepts covered in this chapter. Before assigning these exercises, you may wish to review any parts of the chapter that have proved difficult for many or most of the students. (See Key to Exercises.)

Chapter 5

The Process of Writing Pages 77–83

Objectives

1. To understand that all writing involves the same basic process

2. To study the three major steps in the process of writing: prewriting; writing a first draft; and rewriting, or revising

Introduction

This chapter serves as a transition between the chapters on vocabulary development and sentence writing that precede it and those on paragraph and composition that follow it. This chapter is unique among all the chapters in the book in that it does not provide exercises for which students must apply newly-learned skills. Rather, it is designed so that students must apply their skills in subsequent chapters that focus on specific types of writing.

Part 1

Pre-Writing

Pages 78–79

As you read and discuss the introduction to this section, on page 78, list on the chalkboard the specific activities that make up the pre-writing step (choose a subject, focus on the subject, and so on). Analyze the sample pre-writing notes on page 79, clarifying if necessary, the meanings of *descriptive paragraph*, *third person point of view*, *sensory details*, and *mood*.

Part 2

Writing the First Draft

Page 80

Read and discuss the introductory material and the example of the first draft on page 80. Guide the class in identifying the details from the prewriting notes that the writer incorporated into the first draft. Discourage the students from suggesting ways to improve the paragraph, reminding them that revision is the next step in the process of writing.

Part 3

Rewriting, or Revising

Pages 80–83

Open the discussion of this section by reviewing Handbook Section 17.4 (Correcting Symbols and Revision).

Discuss the points to consider when rewriting, or revising, a piece of writing. Then analyze the changes made by the writer of the sample paragraph. Note that the writer substituted more specific colorful words (for example, *motionless, sweltering* for *hot, thick*; *small, scorched* for *burned-out*; *searched* for *looked at*); added indicators of place (for example, *on Lincoln Street; nearby*); deleted repetitive statements (for example: *She barely had the energy to move her arm; their tempers fueled by the heat*) and clarified ambiguous phrases (for example, *inside the house* rather than *inside*; *for signs of the much-needed rain* instead of *for the much needed rain*). Explain that this type of revision is more difficult and involved than proofreading in which mechanics are checked.

Proofreading. Remind the class that capitalization, punctuation, spelling, and good manuscript form are covered in Handbook Sections 11.0–17.14.

Guidelines for the Process of Writing. Explain that the guidelines on page 83 summarize the steps that have been explained and demonstrated on preceding pages. Check understanding by questioning the students about the three steps and about each activity on the list.

Less-Advanced Students. Refer these students to the chart on page 83 when assigning paragraphs, compositions, and reports. You might want to write the guidelines on a large sheet of poster paper to hang in the classroom; to duplicate the guidelines for the students to keep handy in their notebooks; or to have the students copy the guidelines into their journals.

Advanced Students. After the completion of several writing assignments for exercises in subsequent chapters, these students most likely will have internalized the process of writing so that they will no longer need to refer to this chapter. However, if students begin to hand in paragraphs and compositions that reflect little planning and no revision, review the guidelines on page 83.

Chapter 6

Writing Effective Paragraphs

Pages 85–105

Objectives

1. To understand the requirements for a well written paragraph

2. To understand the function and characteristics of a topic sentence

3. To construct a topic sentence that can be adequately supported or explained by specific detail

Introduction

The paragraph, as a tightly structured form, can be a vehicle through which students learn to organize their thinking. As they learn to write clear, well developed, interesting paragraphs, they will be mastering the form that is the basis for most of the writing they will do throughout their lives.

Part 1

What Is a Paragraph?

Pages 85–93

Discuss the definition of *paragraph* that opens Part 1. Explain that paragraphs that fulfill the requirements stated in the definition are unified and that paragraphs in which the ideas are presented logically are coherent. The terms *unity* and *coherence* (and their derivations) are used frequently in the composition chapters and, therefore, must be clearly understood by all the students.

Example 1. Read the examples and related discussion on page 86. Review the term *chronological order,* using the sample paragraph to illustrate the definition.

Example 2. Review the terms *unity* and *coherence* and introduce the term *order of importance,* using the sample paragraph and related discussion.

Example 3. This paragraph exemplifies a common type of error in which a writer introduces ideas related to the general subject of a paragraph but not to its specific topic. If the students repeatedly have difficulty in detecting this kind of error, direct them when studying a paragraph to check each sentence against the topic sentence to make sure that it is *directly* related to the main idea of the paragraph.

Example 4. Guide the students through the analysis on page 89. If you are not certain that all the students have mastered the key concepts in the lesson, use two or three paragraphs from the exercise on pages 90–93 as the basis for further discussion or as a preliminary evaluation tool.

Exercise. Help the students to analyze several of the groups of sentences on pages 90–93. (See Keys to Exercises.) Then assign the remainder of the exercise as independent work. Encourage students to add information to those paragraphs from which sentences must be deleted. Check the students' writing carefully to make sure that they understand the concept of a unified paragraph. Do not proceed with Part 2 until all students can identify well written paragraphs and the deficiencies in poorly written ones.

Less-Advanced Students. These students may need individual attention while the others are completing the exercise independently.

Advanced Students. These students should have little difficulty in completing the exercise.

Part 2
The Topic Sentence and Its Function
Pages 93–98

A good topic sentence is essential to a well written paragraph because it is the one sentence that controls the content of the entire paragraph. It controls both the supporting ideas and the length of the paragraph.

Example 1. Explain that the controlling idea for this paragraph is the basic limitation of computers, not computers in general, and that this is the idea developed by the supporting sentences.

Example 2. After reading the sample paragraph and related discussion, have the students suggest possible topic sentences that would fit the content of the paragraph.

Key Words. Emphasize again the controlling function of the topic sentence. Have the students change the key words in each sentence to demonstrate their importance in determining content.

Paragraph Length. Students must understand that a paragraph should be as long as is necessary to develop a single idea.

Exercise. Help the students analyze the first two or three paragraphs on pages 96–97. Then assign the remainder of the exercise as independent work.

Less-Advanced Students. These students will need help in analyzing all of the paragraphs. For each paragraph, ask them to identify the main idea, then to check each supporting sentence against that idea.

Advanced Students. The advanced students should be able to complete this exercise without difficulty. You might wish to have them rewrite the poorly written paragraphs, an activity not called for in the directions.

Catching the Reader's Attention. When discussing this section, have the students suggest ways to revise the dull sentences into more interesting paragraph openers.

Part 3

Characteristics of the Topic Sentence

Pages 98–105

Explain to the students that although a topic sentence can appear anywhere in a paragraph, it generally appears as the opening sentence. All of the examples and exercise paragraphs in this text begin with a topic sentence, which is followed by supporting sentences.

A Topic Sentence Is a General Statement. Guide the students through the analyses of the sample paragraphs on pages 99–100. Emphasize that a general statement encompasses all the specific ideas in a paragraph.

A Topic Sentence Is a Limited Statement. Guide the students through the discussion on pages 100–101. Analyze the sample paragraph carefully, making sure that the students understand that the topic sentence is both general and limited.

Exercises. Assign and evaluate Exercises A and B on pages 102 and 103 before proceeding to Exercises C and D. (See Keys to Exercises.) For Exercise C on page 104, you might want to do paragraphs 1 and 2 as a class, demonstrating how a generalization can be drawn from specific details. After the students have completed the exercise, ask volunteers to read their sentences aloud. Encourage the students to respond to the sentences written by their peers. For Exercise D on page 105, you may wish to have the students work in groups to suggest revisions for each other's paragraphs. Supervise the groups and give help where needed.

Less-Advanced Students. It might be necessary for these students to spend more time on the skill of writing good topic sentences. You might work with them in a small group, using Exercises C and D on pages 104–105 as the basis for discussion. Do not proceed to Chapter 7 until all of these students can write a workable topic sentence.

Advanced Students. Encourage these students to share their completed paragraphs with the class, thus giving less-advanced students the opportunity to hear examples of well written paragraphs.

Chapter 7

Developing the Paragraph

Pages 107–129

Objectives

1. To organize and develop a narrative paragraph

2. To organize and develop paragraphs describing persons, places, and things

3. To organize and develop an explanatory paragraph that gives instructions

4. To write explanatory paragraphs developed by each of these methods:
a. Using facts or statistics
b. Using one or more examples
c. Using an incident or an anecdote
d. Using comparisons or contrasts

5. To write a persuasive paragraph in which an opinion is supported with reasons

6. To write a persuasive paragraph in which a proposition is supported by arguments

Introduction

Throughout this chapter the students should be encouraged to become conscious of their audiences, for audience determines appropriate language and the selection of meaningful facts, examples, and experiences. The class should also be taught the differing purposes of narrative, descriptive, explanatory, and persuasive paragraphs, four types of paragraphs explored in this chapter. Refer the students periodically to the "Checklist for Writing Paragraphs" on page 129.

Part 1

The Narrative Paragraph

Pages 107–111

Writing narrative paragraphs is fun for most students because it allows them to relate happenings, real and imaginary, experienced by themselves and their friends. When reading and discussing the sample paragraphs and explanatory material on pages 107–109, note the distinction made between narrative paragraphs that are part of longer pieces of writing and those that stand alone. Emphasize that both types of narratives have the same basic characteristics: they are the telling of events in chronological order. At the top of page 108 pause to note that although professional writers do not necessarily open their narrative paragraphs with topic sentences, the students should continue to begin each paragraph with a general statement.

Exercises. Have the students complete Exercise A on page 109 independently. The following day, discuss their answers, making sure that each person in the class understands that a narrative paragraph is the telling of events. For Exercise B on page 110, encourage the students to be aware of the impressions they wish to create as they write their paragraphs. Caution them to choose subjects that can be treated in one paragraph that is not excessively long.

Less-Advanced Students. Motivate all these students to observe and be sensitive to experiences that might provide material for narrative paragraphs. Use the results of Exercise B to assess needs for individual help.

Advanced Students. These students will need little help in completing the exercises. Because motivation is a primary factor in writing, try to create an atmosphere that will excite and encourage the students to write about their experiences, even when narrative paragraphs are not assigned as class work.

Part 2

The Descriptive Paragraph

Pages 111–116

Good descriptive writing demands that the writer choose words and details carefully in order to paint a word picture that appeals to one or more of the senses. Encourage the students to develop the habit of recording words and phrases with strong sensory appeal, observations, and experiences in journals. (These journals can be used throughout this course of study.)

Organizing Visual Details. Read and discuss the explanation and model paragraphs on pages 113–114. Have the students analyze the spatial order of each paragraph and identify the words and phrases used to indicate direction. As you discuss each model, draw a simple diagram on the chalkboard to show the placement of each item mentioned. Emphasize that direction words are essential to understanding the spatial order in these paragraphs.

Describing a Person. Read and discuss the sample paragraphs and related explanations on pages 114–115. Emphasize the major difference between descriptions of places and things, and descriptions of people: the purpose of one is to create a sense impression of external qualities; the purpose of the other is to capture inner qualities.

Exercises. When assigning Exercise A on page 115, remind the students to make a list of sensory details and to arrange them in some kind of logical order before beginning to write. Some of the topics lend themselves to spatial order. Others can be organized according to sense appeal; that is, the details that appeal to each sense should be grouped together. For Exercise B, have the students focus on two or three qualities rather than attempting to capture the entire person in one paragraph.

Less-Advanced Students. These students will need small group or individual help in using words and phrases with sensory appeal and in identifying and communicating the inner qualities of people. The latter skill may be beyond some students at this level.

Part 3
The Explanatory Paragraph
Pages 116–125

Part 3 examines several different ways of developing explanatory paragraphs. The discussion of each is followed by an exercise that provides practice in writing that particular kind of explanation.

Giving Instructions. Have the students read and discuss the models on pages 116–117. Emphasize the importance of clarity in this type of explanation.

Exercise. Have the students exchange the first drafts of their paragraphs and try out each other's directions before writing final versions to be handed in for evaluation.

Using Facts or Statistics. When discussing the models on page 118, clarify the terms *statistic* and *fact* by asking the students to identify the statistics and facts in the paragraphs.

Exercise. Allow time for the students to research and narrow their topics, providing individual guidance where needed.

Using One or More Examples. Read and discuss the model paragraphs and related explanations on pages 119–120. Note that both paragraphs begin with general statements that are supported with one or more examples.

Exercise. When assigning the exercise on page 120, point out that the list of subjects is meant to give students ideas for specific topics and that their topic sentences must be limited statements that can be developed in one paragraph.

Using an Incident or an Anecdote. Clarify for the class the differences and similarities between this type of paragraph, an explanatory paragraph developed by one example, and a narrative paragraph.

Exercises. Provide time for the students to share their completed paragraphs with the class. Point out how each general statement was personalized by an incident or anecdote unique to the writer.

Using Comparisons or Contrasts. To reinforce the concepts of comparison and contrast, have the students identify the specific similarities and differences described in the paragraphs.

Exercises. For Exercise A, most of the subjects lend themselves equally well to development by comparison or contrast; the choices depend on the writer's point of view. Display the sample explanatory paragraphs brought in for Exercise B on a bulletin board, along with phrases or sentences that describe the method of development used by each writer.

Less-Advanced Students. These students will need individual help in completing the exercises in Part 3.

Advanced Students. These students may wish to bring more than one example of an explanatory paragraph to class for discussion. They should have little trouble completing the assignments in Part 3; therefore, they should concentrate on polishing and refining their writing skills.

Part 4
The Persuasive Paragraph
Pages 125–129

When studying Part 4, it is important for the students to keep in mind that while they may have valid reasons for believing as they do, others may have equally valid reasons for believing as *they* do. The persuasive paragraph gives students the opportunity to express their personal beliefs on debatable or controversial topics.

Giving Opinions and Reasons. Review the difference between a fact and an opinion, using the sample paragraph and related explanation on pages 125–126. Emphasize that the purpose of such a paragraph is to present convincing reasons in support of an opinion.

Stating Propositions and Supporting Arguments. Emphasize the difference in purpose between this type of persuasive paragraph and the first type. Note the importance of facts in supporting a proposition of belief. Ask the students to explain in their own words each of the three "things to keep in mind" listed at the bottom of page 127. You might want to cut out several well written editorials and letters to the editor from newspapers and magazines and to read them to the class as examples of this type of persuasive paragraph. Guide students in analyzing the method of development used by each writer.

Exercises. For Exercise A on page 128, have each student state the purpose of his or her paragraph. Provide time for the students to share their completed paragraphs with their peers. Direct the class to evaluate each paragraph on the basis of how well it fulfills its stated purpose. Have the students also comment on the strength and weakness of the reasons or arguments used in each paragraph. Remind the students, when completing Exercise B, to write a topic sentence that is sufficiently limited to be developed in one paragraph.

Checklist for Writing Paragraphs. Encourage the students to use this checklist as a tool for revising their paragraphs.

Less-Advanced Students. Work with these students as they prepare to write their paragraphs for Exercises A and B. Provide guidance in choosing a subject, in writing an opinion or proposition of belief (for Exercise B), and in making a list of possible supporting details to include in the paragraph.

Advanced Students. These students may wish to write about controversial community or national issues. Instruct them to gather information from newspapers and magazines in support of both sides of the issues before writing their propositions of belief.

Chapter 8

Writing a Composition or a Report

Pages 131–165

Objectives

1. To understand the structure of a composition in relation to the structure of a paragraph

2. To choose a subject and to narrow that subject into a specific topic appropriate for development in a five-paragraph composition

3. To become aware of the influence of audience and purpose on the content and language of a composition

4. To develop a plan for a composition

5. To write a five-paragraph composition that has an introductory paragraph, a body, and a conclusion

Introduction

This chapter deals with the specific steps involved in writing a composition or report. In Chapters 6 and 7 the students studied paragraph writing; they learned many of the basic skills that are needed for development of any well constructed piece of writing. Take every opportunity to remind the students that they are building on and extending skills that they have already mastered.

Part 1

What Is a Composition?

Pages 131–133

Compare and contrast the definition of a composition with that of a paragraph. Emphasize the similarity in function between the topic sentence of a paragraph and the introductory paragraph of a composition. Point out that just as all the sentences in a paragraph must relate directly to the topic sentence, all the paragraphs in a composition must relate to the introductory paragraph. Discuss the model on pages 132–133, using the explanatory paragraphs that follow the model as the basis for your discussion.

Less-Advanced Students. These students should be helped to understand how an introductory paragraph controls the content of a composition.

Advanced Students. Ask these students to bring in articles from magazines that have strong introductory paragraphs and well developed supporting paragraphs. Discuss each article, having the students identify the one main idea of the article, describe the way that the introductory paragraph presents that idea, and explain the role of the supporting paragraphs in developing the main idea.

Part 2
Deciding on a Subject
Pages 133–138

Encourage the students to write about subjects that interest them. Explain that if a teacher assigns an unappealing topic, they should try to find one aspect of the subject that they can explore with some degree of interest.

Subjects That Relate to Personal Experience. Reinforce at this time the importance of keeping a journal to record ideas, impressions, sensations, and feelings that might be used later as a resource for writing. The model on pages 134–135 is a good example of how a person's own experience can provide an interesting and worthwhile subject for a composition. Some classes might benefit from reviewing the definition of a composition, using this composition as the basis for analysis and discussion.

Exercise. Have the students complete the exercise on page 135, reminding them to keep their lists for future reference.

Subjects Outside the Writer's Experience. Discuss the material on pages 136–137, stressing the sources of information that are available when writing a composition of this kind. Note the necessity for becoming familiar with a subject before writing about it.

Exercises. Have the students complete Exercise A on page 137, reminding them to keep their lists for future reference. If you decide to have all the students work on topics that require library research, direct the class, when assigning Exercise B on page 138, to choose a subject from the list completed for Exercise A. (See *Less-Advanced Students* below.)

Less-Advanced Students. You may want to have these students choose subjects that relate to personal experiences, thus eliminating the need for library research.

Advanced Students. These students should have no difficulty in completing the exercises in part 2.

Part 3
Narrowing the Subject

Pages 138–141

Help the students analyze the material on pages 138–139. Make sure that they understand the difference between a broad subject and a specific topic. If the class seems to be having difficulty with this concept, refer the students to the Tables of Contents of several textbooks. Point out the chapter titles as examples of broad subjects and the headings of short sections as examples of specific topics.

The Narrowing Process. Read and discuss the instructions on pages 139–141. Emphasize the two steps involved in narrowing a subject that requires research: (1) locating books on the subject and (2) checking the Tables of Contents for topic ideas.

Exercise. If possible, make arrangements for a class visit to the school library so that you will be available to provide guidance as the students complete the exercise on page 141.

Less-Advanced Students. Help these students select books on their subjects. If necessary, review library procedures, using Chapter 11, Using Library and Reference Works, pages 231–249 of this text.

Advanced Students. These students may tend to choose topics that are too broad for five-paragraph compositions. Help them to narrow their focuses to specific topics.

Part 4

Deciding on the Audience and the Purpose

Pages 141–143

Sensitivity to audience and awareness of purpose are essential for good writing, for it is these two factors that determine the language and content of a composition.

1. **Know your audience.** Discuss the material on pages 141–142. Encourage the students to point out words and ideas that indicate the audience of each model paragraph. To further clarify the concept, discuss the type of vocabulary that might be used to describe the weather in each of these pieces of writing: a letter to an elderly relative, a letter to a good friend, a report for a tenth grade science class, a technical journal for professional weather forecasters, and a poem for young children.

2. **Know your purpose for writing.** Discuss the material on pages 142–143. At this point you may wish to explain briefly the terms *tone* and *mood*. Tone is the writer's attitude toward a subject; mood is the way the *reader* feels about what he or she has read. The tone and mood of a composition are not necessarily identical. For example, a writer's attitude toward a subject (tone) can be straight-forward and matter-of-fact, but the reader could feel a sense of terror (mood).

Exercises. You may wish to assist students in completing the exercises on page 143. You could have them describe their audiences and purposes in writing or orally, depending on the size and make-up of the class.

Less-Advanced Students. Distribute materials of various levels, from first grade up through technical journals. Have the students list the name of each book or magazine and indicate its probable audience. The purposes of the articles might also be discussed. Help the students to recognize differences in vocabulary, sentence structure, and complexity of ideas among the examples.

Advanced Students. Help these students to pinpoint as specifically as possible the audiences and purposes of their compositions.

Part 5

Planning the Composition

Pages 143–151

It is important that the students realize that a well written composition does not just "happen." It requires careful planning, the end product of which is an outline that will serve as a guide for writing. The four essential steps in the planning process examined in Part 5 are these:

1. Gathering information
2. Grouping ideas
3. Making a working outline
4. Organizing the composition

Gathering Information. Whether the students are writing a composition based on personal experience or one based on learned information, they will use the same method for recording ideas. Remind the class to continue to record ideas in their journals.

Finding and Recording Information. The instructions in this section apply only to those students who need to research their composition topics. Go over the material on pages 144–146 with this group, emphasizing the following directions: record the identifying information for each source on 3" x 5" cards; assign a number to each source so that ideas taken from that source can be easily identified; record one idea on each note card. If necessary, review the use of the *Readers' Guide to Periodical Literature*, using the material on pages 245–246 of this text.

Exercise. Allow the students several days to complete the exercise on page 146. Check note cards daily to be sure that they conform to the criteria set forth in the preceding two sections.

Grouping Ideas. Help the students to understand the process described on pages 146–147. Emphasize that although grouping ideas is often difficult, it is a necessary step in the planning process.

Exercises. Work with the entire class to complete Exercise A on page 147. (See Keys to Exercises.) When you are certain that all of the students understand the difference between general and specific headings, assign Exercise B on page 148. (See Keys to Exercises.) As you correct this exercise with the class, identify those students who need additional help. Work with them in a small group. Then assign Exercise C on page 148.

You might want to have the students work in small groups to discuss their ideas and the proper grouping of them. Move from group to group, giving help where needed.

Making a Working Outline. Help the students to understand the material on pages 148–149. While organizing paragraphs in chronological order and in order of importance is familiar to the students, organizing a greater number of ideas may prove to be difficult. You might want to review the third basic type of order—spatial order—which is not discussed in the text. Remind the students that the ideas in descriptive writing are often arranged in this order.

Exercises. Exercise A on page 150 should be completed on the chalkboard so that all students can follow the development of a working outline. (See Keys to Exercises.) Note that number 1 has one heading; number 2 has two headings; and number 3 has three headings and is a sentence outline. Students should copy the completed outlines and keep them as a reference. When you are satisfied that the students understand the process of organizing ideas, assign Exercise B on page 151. Evaluate the students' outlines carefully.

Organizing the Composition. Be sure that the students understand the way that a working outline becomes part of a final outline. If necessary, review correct outline form with the class. (See Handbook, Section 18.4, pages 533–534.)

Exercise. Check the students' completed outlines for form and content. Work with those students whose outlines will not serve as clear guides for writing their compositions.

Less-Advanced Students. Organizing ideas seems to be the most difficult task for these students. Therefore, your patience and positive reinforcement are especially important at this time. If possible, encourage the students to come in during free periods and after school for help.

Advanced Students. Urge these students to research a variety of sources, including interviews with experts, when preparing the content of their compositions.

Part 6

Writing the Composition

Pages 152–165

After you have checked the students' outlines, begin discussing the process of writing the three parts of a composition.

The Introductory Paragraph. Discuss the material on page 152 and the top of page 153. Emphasize the twofold function of an introductory paragraph: to indicate the content of a composition and to catch the reader's attention. Draw parallels between an introductory paragraph of a composition and the topic sentence of a paragraph. Then discuss the different types of introductory paragraphs, using the models and related explanation on pages 153–154.

Exercises. Exercise A on page 154 is based on the concept that one sentence, usually the opening sentence, of an introductory paragraph states the main idea of that paragraph and, therefore, of the entire composition. For Exercise B, you may wish to have the students work in groups to exchange ideas about effective introductory paragraphs for their compositions.

The Body. Read and discuss pages 155–158 with the students, making sure that they understand the function and organization of the body of a composition. Refer the class to the outline on pages 148–149 to illustrate how the writer of the sample composition followed the outline when writing the body paragraphs of the composition. Emphasize that a composition is always divided into paragraphs and that each paragraph usually begins with a topic sentence. Have the students look over their own outlines to see how their compositions will be divided into paragraphs. Discuss the achievement of unity in a composition, using the folktale, the final composition in this section, as the basis for discussion.

Transitional Devices. Examine with the students the paragraphs that illustrate the use of transitional devices on pages 158–160. You may wish to have the students circle the transitional words and phrases in the first drafts of their compositions, thus helping them to become aware of the devices that they use unconsciously to tie their ideas together.

Giving Credit. Caution the students to give credit for direct quotations. Explain that they will give general credit to their sources at the end of their compositions.

Exercises. Exercise A on pages 161–163 can be completed as class work. (See Keys to Exercises.) Exercise B should be completed individually. Encourage the students to have classmates read their papers and make suggestions for revisions.

The Conclusion. Read and discuss the material on pages 163–164, emphasizing the variety of approaches that may be taken when writing the ending of a composition.

Exercise. Encourage the students to experiment with different conclusions before writing a final version. You might have them list their sources after the conclusions of their compositions.

Rewriting, or Revising. Have the students revise and proofread their completed compositions, using the Checklist for Writing Compositions or Reports on page 165, the steps for proofreading at the bottom of page 83, and the Handbook section of the text.

Collect the best examples of the students' compositions and put them together into a class "literary magazine." Duplicate and distribute the magazine among your students.

Less-Advanced Students. Schedule time to work individually with these students at each step of the writing process. By completing a segment of the paper at a time, the whole composition will not seem so overwhelming.

Advanced Students. These students most likely can follow the procedures in the text with little guidance. It is advisable, however, to check their papers along the way so that they do not become careless or skip a procedure.

Chapter 9

Types of Compositions Pages 167–201

Objectives

1. To study the characteristics of narrative, descriptive, explanatory, and persuasive compositions

2. To apply the procedures for writing a composition to the four types of compositions studied in this chapter

3. To understand point of view and the techniques used to achieve unity, coherence, and emphasis and to apply this knowledge in writing the four types of compositions

Introduction

The four basic types of compositions examined in this chapter comprise most of the writing required of students throughout high school and college. Most of your students will have had some experience in writing each type, although they may not be aware of it. The students also will bring to these lessons a familiarity with narrative, descriptive, explanatory, and persuasive paragraphs, which will serve as the basis for writing these kinds of compositions. As you proceed through the chapter, do not hesitate to refer to preceding chapters, primarily Chapters 7 and 8, to review points that may have been forgotten by the students.

Part 1
The Narrative Composition

Pages 167–185

Begin the study of narrative writing by reading and discussing the explanation on pages 167–169. These paragraphs explain in some detail the three basic elements of all narrative writing—character, setting, and conflict. They also clarify the difference between a simple narrative and a complex narrative.

Unity, Coherence, and Emphasis. This section continues the discussion of characteristics present in both simple and complex narratives. If necessary, review transitional devices (see Chapter 8, pages 158–160) and the concept of chronological order.

The Simple Narrative. Guide the class through the reading and analysis of the simple narrative on pages 169–171. Note the highly descriptive language used throughout the composition and explain briefly that descriptive language is not confined to descriptive paragraphs and compositions, but is found in all types of good writing.

Point of View. Introduce the concept of point of view, using the explanation on pages 171–172. Note that the simple narrative on page 170 employs first person point of view with the narrator being a participant in the action. The text presents many complex ideas in a few paragraphs. Therefore, you may wish to supplement the explanation with examples of paragraphs that illustrate the various approaches to point of view. You might ask the advanced students in your class to locate these examples.

Exercise. For the exercise on page 173, allow the students several days to organize, write, and revise their narratives.

Less-Advanced Students. These students might have difficulty choosing and implementing a point of view and evaluating whether their compositions are characterized by unity, coherence, and emphasis. Provide individual and small-group guidance throughout the process of completing the exercise.

Advanced Students. Give these students practice in exercising control over their writing by having them write their narratives from two different points of view, then evaluate which point of view is the most effective.

The Complex Narrative or Short Story. Read and discuss pages 173–174, where the characteristics of a well written short story are described. Assure the students that the ideas presented on these pages will be clearer after studying an example of a complex narrative.

Story 1. Allow time for two reading of this story, as suggested in the introduction to the story on page 174.

Analysis. Proceed carefully through the analysis on pages 178–179. Whenever possible, have the students read the sentence or paragraph in which the element or characteristic is evident—for example, the sentence in which the setting is established and the paragraph in which the climax is reached.

Story 2. Allow time for the two readings of this story suggested in the introduction on page 179.

Analysis. Discuss the analysis on pages 184–185 with the class. Point out that this story exhibits the five characteristics listed on pages 173–174.

Exercises. For Exercise A on page 185, give the class the following specific directions:

1. Identify the main character or characters.
2. Identify any minor characters.
3. Give the time framework, if possible.
4. Describe the place where the story takes place.
5. Describe the point of view chosen by the writer.
6. Describe the techniques employed for achieving unity.
7. Describe the techniques employed for achieving coherence.
8. Describe the techniques employed for achieving emphasis.
9. Explain how the story evidences all or some of the five characteristics listed on pages 173–174.

When assigning Exercise B, emphasize the importance of developing an outline before beginning to write. Remind the class that the short story is a highly structured, tightly woven form and that it should exhibit the five characteristics described on pages 173–174.

Less Advanced Students. Some of these students may write extremely creative stories with little structure. Work individually with them to improve their outlines and revise their narratives.

Advanced Students. Help these students to tighten the structures of their stories and to sharpen details when revising their narratives.

Part 2
The Descriptive Composition
Pages 186–191

Point of view, unity, coherence, and emphasis have been presented in relation to narrative writing. In this section, their specific meanings in relation to descriptive writing are examined.

Point of View. Read and discuss the material on pages 186–187. Contrast the meaning of *point of view* in a narrative composition and in a description. Emphasize that physical point of view should be consistent throughout a descriptive composition, unless a shift in point of view is clearly indicated. Elicit from the class several additional examples of scenes that could be described from different mental points of view.

Unity, Coherence, and Emphasis. Encourage the students to use a thesaurus when selecting words to create precise details. You might explain that a synonym for *coherence* is "clarity" and ask the students to describe the probable reaction of a reader to a composition in which the details are not arranged in logical order.

The Practical Description. Ask the students for a definition of the word *practical*. After a definition is decided upon, with the help of a dictionary if necessary, have the students read the composition on pages 188–189 as an example of a practical description. Guide them through the analysis that follows it.

Exercise. Allow time for the students to do any necessary research on their topics. Remind them to be as objective as possible when writing their descriptions; their mental points of view should not be evident to their readers.

Less-Advanced Students. Encourage these students to choose local attractions as the topics for their compositions and to "research" them by observing their external characteristics.

Advanced Students. Some of these students might wish to describe purely imaginary scenes.

The Artistic Description, or Personal Essay. Read aloud for the class the model on pages 190–191 so that the students can react to its emotional content. The short story "Silent Snow, Secret Snow" by Conrad Aiken is a piece of writing that contains a large amount of artistic description. You might want to read sections of this story to the class.

Exercise. Study several pairs of practical and artistic descriptions with the class to emphasize the difference between the two types of descriptions.

Less-Advanced Students. Remind these students periodically to refer to the twelve steps for writing a composition listed on page 165.

Advanced Students. Encourage these students to be as creative as possible in their writing and to look continually for ways to sharpen their use of descriptive language.

Part 3
The Explanatory Composition
Pages 192–197

When introducing this section, emphasize the importance of mastering the explanatory form of writing, for the students will be writing this type of composition in history, science, and English class throughout their junior and senior years.

The Practical Explanatory Composition. Review the meaning of the word *practical*. Emphasize that this type of composition is characterized by objectivity. After reading the model on pages 193–194, use the questions in Exercise A on page 194 to discuss the techniques used by the writer to achieve unity, coherence, and emphasis.

Exercise. Complete Exercise A on pages 194 and 195 as an oral class activity. For Exercise B, allow time for the students to organize, write, and revise their compositions. Encourage them to choose topics that will require only minimal research.

The Artistic Explanatory Composition, or Essay. Read the model on pages 195–197 aloud to illustrate the emotional appeal of this type of writing.

Exercises. Discuss thoroughly the students' answers for Exercise A. There will probably be considerable variation among the phrases cited for their emotional appeal. For Exercise B, you might want to work in small groups to help students choose topics appropriate for artistic explanatory compositions. Provide time for the students to share their completed essays. After each essay is read, evaluate the writer's achievment of unity, coherence, and emphasis, and his or her skill in choosing words with strong emotional appeal.

Less-Advanced Students. You might want to specify a length of one page for the artistic explanations written by these students. Use the results of Exercise B to identify those students who need individual help.

Advanced Students. The major problem with these students may be the excessive length of their compositions. You may be required to set a maximum length of, perhaps, two pages on their artistic explanations.

Part 4

The Persuasive Composition

Pages 197–201

Read and discuss the explanatory material on pages 197–198. Emphasize the similarities between the persuasive paragraph and the persuasive composition in both intent and structure. Encourage the students to approach this type of composition as an extension of material with which they are already somewhat familiar.

Guide the students in examining the brief on page 199. Note the tight structuring of the composition—each argument supports the conclusion and is backed by supporting information. Emphasize the importance of outlining to a solid, well organized presentation. After reading and discussing the model on page 200, you might want to guide the students in outlining the ideas contained in that composition.

Exercise. Allow time for the students to find material to support their propositions. Encourage them to use the vertical file in order to save time and to consult the *Readers' Guide to Periodical Literature* for current articles. Many students may find that their topics are too broad for a five-paragraph composition. Help each of them to list several narrower topics that are contained within the broad subject, and then to choose one as a final topic. Students should be required to turn in their briefs, or outlines, with their completed compositions.

Less-Advanced Students. These students should select simple topics that can be easily supported. You will want to approve their topics and to help them select and organize their supportive material.

Advanced Students. Have these students find good examples of persuasive compositions in newspapers, magazines, and collections of essays. Discuss with them the organization and presentation of material in these compositions.

Chapter 10

Letters, Applications, and Résumés

Pages 203–229

Objectives

1. To review the forms for writing business letters

2. To review the correct form for addressing a business envelope

3. To distinguish among various kinds of business letters:
    Letters requesting information
    Letters about employment
    Letters to colleges or other schools

4. To learn guidelines for filling out application forms

5. To organize and write a résumé

Introduction

Introduce this chapter by talking about the career choices that students will be making in the near future. Discuss ways in which they can get information about employment opportunities, training programs, and colleges and other schools. A realization of the importance of letter writing should emerge from this discussion.

It is suggested that students keep carbons of all the writing done for this chapter in a folder for future reference.

Part 1

The Forms of Letters

Pages 204–208

Using the examples and explanation on pages 204–208, discuss the six main parts of a business letter. Note details of capitalization and punctuation for each part.

Exercises. After the students have completed Exercise A on page 208, ask volunteers to write the addresses on the chalkboard while the rest of the class checks their own papers. Then have the students complete Exercise B and turn it in for evaluation. (See Key to Exercises.)

Less-Advanced Students. Because it is important to find meaningful letter-writing situations for these students, they might be asked to investigate community employment resources and to use one as the basis for Exercise B.

Advanced Students. These students may be instructed to apply for an actual job at a park or summer camp. Require them to find out who is in charge of the program and the correct address of the organization.

Part 2
The Envelopes
Pages 208–211

Emphasize the importance of addressing envelopes correctly. Explain that the envelope creates the first impression when a letter is received and that an envelope with an incorrect address may not even be delivered to the intended receiver. Many times important requests are not received by the person who can fulfill them. Therefore you should stress the need to find out exactly who should receive a letter. After you are certain that students understand the correct form for writing a business letter and how to addresss an envelope properly, proceed to the exercises on page 211.

Exercises. For Exercise A, allow time for the students to locate the correct addresses. Exercise B will give students an opportunity to be creative in writing a letter. It will also indicate whether the concepts in Parts 1 and 2 have been mastered.

Less-Advanced Students. These students will need reinforcement and encouragement in completing the exercises. Stress the importance of making an impression through a letter and of writing correct and concise letters.

Advanced Students. These students may be assigned to write a business letter to the school paper, either praising the administration, teachers, or students for a new policy that has been adopted, or criticizing an activity or policy that is currently in effect. Make sure that the students use the proper form for their letters and envelopes.

Part 3
Kinds of Business Letters
Pages 212–220

Students should be made aware of the many kinds of letters that people can write to accomplish a wide variety of purposes. This part of the chapter will explain basic guidelines for three different types of letters.

Letters Requesting Information. Remind students to be brief and direct when writing letters requesting information. Stress the three W's (*What*, *Why*, and *When*) as something for the students to remember when writing the bodies of their letters.

General Requests for Information. Many students may feel it is an imposition to write to agencies for information for a school assignment. Assure them that large agencies have employees whose only job is to prepare and distribute informational material.

Exercise. Suggest businesses, government agencies, newspapers, radio and television stations, and associations as sources of information. Provide time for the students to share their letters with the class.

Less-Advanced Students. These students may have difficulty in locating appropriate addresses. You might help them find addresses in the telephone book or you might suggest getting help from a librarian.

Advanced Students. These students may write two letters for the exercise. One could be a request for an interview with someone who might provide information on the subject they have chosen.

Letters About Employment. Most tenth-grade students will be looking ahead to temporary and part-time jobs within the next couple of years. Therefore, they will be easily motivated to be interested in writing this type of letter. As you discuss the material on pages 214–216, encourage students to question points that are not clear.

Exercise. You may want to have the students peruse the help wanted ads in the local newspaper for letter-writing ideas.

Letters to Colleges and Other Schools. College may seem uncertain or far away for tenth-grade students. You should point out, though, that it is never to early to think about what they might like to do. Help students analyze the material on pages 217–219. The paragraph at the top of page 220 suggests that students look into scholarship possibilities. This is an excellent idea, which you should encourage. The school placement office or a counselor might be able to provide you with a list of places for students to write for information.

Exercise. Refer students to catalogs for colleges, universities, and vocational schools, which are available in the library or in the school placement office.

Less-Advanced Students. Remind these students to be sure that they have included the three W's in their letters. Go over the letters and envelopes carefully for form and content before mailing them.

Advanced Students. Have these students request information from a foundation about grants available to high school students for field work in a particular area of study.

Part 4
Application Forms
Pages 220–223

Students will be filling out innumerable forms during the course of their lifetimes. It is therefore important that they learn to read instructions carefully, to follow directions precisely, and to answer questions accurately. Because most students have a tendency either to underestimate themselves or to exaggerate their abilities, you should remind them repeatedly to answer all questions on an application as honestly as possible.

Exercise. The exercise on pages 221–223 provides an opportunity for students to practice answering the kinds of questions found on application forms.

Less-Advanced Students. These students may need help with some of the vocabulary on the application forms. Provide individual help as needed or assign an advanced student to work with each less-advanced student in completing the exercise.

Advanced Students. Suggest that these students obtain college applications from the counseling office and practice filling them out.

Part 5

Résumés

Pages 224–229

To stimulate introspection on the part of students, ask them to write autobiographies that include the following information: family background, interests, significant experiences, and personal beliefs and values.

Work with the students as they follow the instructions on pages 225 and 226 for developing a worksheet. Less-advanced students particularly may need help in determining objectives. Encourage them to consider a wide variety of fields that reflect their interests. These might range from mountain climbing to auto mechanics to marine biology. After the students have completed their worksheets, discuss the instructions for revision presented on page 228.

Exercise. The exercise on page 228 includes a model for writing a résumé. Walk around the room as the students are working on their résumés to make sure that they are using this model as a guide.

Less-Advanced Students. Remind these students that résumés list only basic information about a person's qualifications, goals, and experience. Emphasize that a résumé is not a personal form, and that students might be asked to write an autobiography to accompany this form or to answer additional personal questions.

Advanced Students. Have these students gather at least five sample résumés from books about résumé writing or from adults they know. Discuss with them which résumés are most appealing and effective and why.

Chapter 11

Using the Library and Reference Works

Objectives

1. To review the classification and arrangement of fiction and nonfiction books

2. To review the use of the card catalog and the *Readers' Guide to Periodical Literature*

3. To review nine different types of reference works: dictionaries; encyclopedias; almanacs and yearbooks; biographical references; books about authors; literary reference books; pamphlets, handbooks, and catalogs; atlases; and magazines

Introduction

The farther along students are in school, the more they will need to use the library. Although the students have most likely been taught the basic library skills, many have avoided the library during their freshman year. It is important, therefore, to spend several days reviewing the use of the library and to arrange for students to gain practical library experience.

Reminder. Plan in advance with the librarian for class visits to the library during which students can work on the exercises in this chapter.

Part 1
How Books are Classified and Arranged
Pages 232–234

The Classification of Books. Review first the two broad categories of books: fiction and nonfiction. Elicit examples of both from the students. Then spend some time discussing the Dewey Decimal System for classifying nonfiction books. Supplement the material in the text with samples of nonfiction books, several of which are on the same subject.

Ask the students to identify the category in which each would be classified. Show the students the call numbers on the spines of the books. Note that each category is subdivided, a fact that can be deduced by examining the call numbers of the books on the same subject.

Arrangement of Books on the Shelves. Explain that libraries arrange books differently; for example, some libraries shelve collections of short stories separately from other fiction books. Have the students compare the arrangement of books in the nearest public library with that in the school library. (If you assign this activity, be sure to warn the school librarian about the possible influx of students visiting the library before and after school hours.)

Exercises. Exercises A and B can be completed as class activities. If a question arises about the classification of an item, send a student to the library to verify the category. (See Key to Exercises.)

After studying the classification and arrangement of books, arrange to spend a class period in the library. Ask the librarian to show the students the vertical file, various indices, films, recordings, and the globe. Whenever possible, stagger subsequent library activities so that congestion is kept to a minimum.

Less-Advanced Students. Throughout this chapter, work on developing the confidence of these students in using the library as a source for many different types of useful information.

Advanced Students. These students could be shown the locations of more sophisticated materials; for example: professional journals and reserved books.

Part 2

Using the Card Catalog

Pages 235–240

As you read aloud the opening paragraphs in this section, be certain that the students understand the terms *card catalog* and *call number*. Tenth graders probably have used the card catalog during their ninth-grade year, but you may find that many students have forgotten what it contains and where it is located.

Using the samples on pages 235 and 236, point out the differences between an author card, a title card, and a subject card. Cite several examples of times when each is useful and ask the class to contribute additional examples.

A few students may need to review the filing system in the card catalog. Explain that cards are filed alphabetically, with the author card filed under the author's last name, the title card filed under the first important word in the title, and the subject card filed under the first word in the subject. Note that books whose titles begin with *a, an,* and *the* are alphabetized under the second word in the title; for example, the title card for *A Bell for Adano* would be filed under *B* for *Bell.*

The location of the title on a card might also confuse many students. Use the sample cards on pages 235 and 236 to point out where the title appears on each type of card.

Card Information. Some students may be unaware of the kind of additional information found on author, title, and subject cards. Review the explanation on page 237 and ask the students to identify the extra information on the sample cards in the text.

Cross Reference Cards. Note that the *Readers' Guide* and encyclopedias also use cross references. Advise the students that cross references are particularly helpful when they need specific information on a narrow topic within a general subject area.

Guide Cards. Mention that not all subjects are listed on guide cards. These cards are in the card catalog to aid students in locating general subject headings.

Exercises. Exercise A should be completed as independent work. You might need to explain that the groups of words in italics are the titles of books. Give the class several days to complete Exercises B, C, and D to avoid overcrowding at the card catalog. (See Key to Exercises.)

Less-Advanced Students. These students may have difficulty with the cross reference cards. If possible, when the class is working in the library, spend time with them, showing them various examples of how these cards are used.

Advanced Students. Challenge these students to find cross reference cards with a large number of references. Discuss briefly the value of investigating cross references when gathering material for a report.

Part 3

Using Reference Works

Pages 240–249

Because teachers in other departments may assume that students already are familiar with reference books, they sometimes fail to review the use of these books before assigning a report or a project. It is therefore up to you, the English teacher, to introduce the students to such material. This section reviews the titles of reference works that may have been studied during the ninth-grade year. The emphasis is on the variety of reference material available in most libraries.

If for some reason it is impossible for the class to use the library, reference books might be checked out and displayed in the classroom so that all students can become familiar with them. Even if the class is able to visit the library as a group, it may be worthwhile to have these materials in the classroom.

1. **Dictionaries.** The dictionary is the students' most important reference book. If you do not have a dictionary for each student, borrow copies from other teachers to use when introducing dictionary skills. Classrooms often contain a variety of dictionaries, some new and some old. This is an advantage rather than a disadvantage, for if students are familiar with only one dictionary, they often have difficulty adapting their skills to others. (Note: the *Thorndike-Barnhart High School Dictionary* contains more simplified definitions than *The Webster's New Collegiate Dictionary*.)

Many students believe that the sole purpose of a dictionary is to assist with defining, spelling, and syllabicating words. Counter this assumption by showing the students the many different kinds of information that can be found in a dictionary's appendices.

Show the students the location of the unabridged dictionary in the school library. Explain that unabridgeddictionaries contain sentences for each entry. These might be helpful when the students study vocabulary words, for they can see these words used in their proper contexts.

Also show the students several examples of specific-subject dictionaries If possible, these should include *A Dictionary of Slang and Unconventional English*, which is guaranteed to be popular with the class.

Encourage the students to bring condensed spelling dictionaries to class or at least to keep them at home. A 50,000-word pocket dictionary is so much easier to use than an eight pound collegiate dictionary, that students are more likely to use it to check the spellings of words.

2. **Encyclopedias.** Encyclopedias can be an excellent first source to which students may turn, for these books present overviews of both general and specific subjects and contain cross references to other entries and to related materials. Emphasize the inadvisability of plagiarizing encyclopedia articles or parts of articles.

3. **Almanacs and Yearbooks.** Listed in this section are some of the most popular and interesting reference works for teenagers. Tenth graders are often fascinated by the unusual information found in books such as the *Guinness Book of World Records* and the *World Almanac and Book of Facts*.

4. **Biographical References.** You may prefer to discuss these books in detail at a later date, when the students require their use for reports on authors and famous persons. However, it is wise to introduce these types of books with the other reference materials in case other teachers assign reports on famous (and infamous) persons.

5. **Books About Authors.** These reference works are particularly valuable for students in an Englich class, for knowing an author's background can assist them in interpreting the author's works.

Students should be instructed on the use of some of these reference books. For example, *Contemporary Authors* is comprised of more than twenty volumes. The index, which is the last volume, refers the students to the specific vloume in which material on a particular author can be found. Warn the class that these reference books are limited; they do not include every author who lived during a specific period and some cover a relatively short time span.

6. **Literary Reference Books.** These books are most useful when students want to use quotations from literary materials in their speeches and expository papers.

7. **Pamphlets, Handbooks, and Catalogs.** If the school library does not have a vertical file, encourage the librarian to begin to compile material for such a file. Many tenth-grade students will not attempt to use a vertical file unless you strongly urge its use. After they discover how simple it is to use, however, they will most likely continue to use it.

8. **Atlases.** To reinforce the fact that atlases are more than collections of maps, have the students locate interesting and unusual facts in a class-

room atlas. Note that libraries generally have a variety of atlases, which should be explored by the students on their next library visit.

9. **Magazines.** Periodicals rank second to dictionaries as important sources of information for students at all ability levels. When discussing the material on pages 245 and 246, stress the following points:

a. Because students often forget to list the page number of a specific article, they waste time in locating it. Instruct them to record not only the title and date of the magazine, but also the page numbers of the article.

b. Cross references, mentioned earlier in this manual, can help students find articles on various subjects. For example, most students would look under "Child abuse" when seeking material on that subject; there they would find a cross reference to "Cruelty to children" under which the articles on this subject are listed. Encourage the students to ask a librarian for assistance when they are unable to find certain subjects.

c. Even though the *Readers' Guide* lists more than 100 magazines, this does not mean that the school library subscribes to all of them. Students can save time by consulting the list of periodicals available in the school library.

Exercises. Divide the class into five groups and assign one of the five exercises to each group. After the groups have completed these exercises, assign a second exercise to each group, and so on until all the students have completed the five exercises.

For Exercise A, caution the students to write a brief report, which summarizes the material in the three encyclopedias. For Exercise C, you might allow the past five or six years' issues to be used rather than only the current issue. (See Keys to Exercises.)

Less-Advanced Students. You might want to reduce the number of items in each exercise assigned to these students.

Advanced Students. Have these students locate reference books in the library that are not mentioned in this chapter.

Chapter 12

Group Discussion Pages 251-257

Objectives

1. To understand the duties of a chairperson and a participant

2. To analyze a sample group discussion

3. To have an opportunity to participate in a group discussion

Introduction

People talk over the telephone, in the halls at school, at the dinner table, in their cars, in the lunchroom, on the street, and in the classroom. In short, they discuss and converse everywhere and nearly all the time.

There is fine line between discussion and conversation. In this chapter, the term *discussion* is loosely used to cover almost any interchange of ideas. The chapter focuses specifically on *informal discussion*, which is actually a combination of discussion and conversation.

A study of this chapter will enable the students to work with others who perhaps do not share the same views, to take a logical approach to the solution of problems, and to communicate effectively in groups.

Your Duties as Chairperson

Pages 251-252

Every student in the class should know the duties of both the chairperson and the participant, for situations will occur in which they will need to exercise both skills. The chairperson has the most difficult job because if the discussion falters in any way, it is the duty of that person to guide the group back into a fruitful and interesting exchange of ideas.

1. **Prepare for the discussion.** One of the discussion plans commonly employed by decision-making groups is based on John Dewey's five basic steps: (a) defining the problem, (b) analyzing the problem, (c) suggesting solutions, (d) evaluating the solutions, and (e) putting the preferred solution into effect. These five steps have been used for years in training

chairpersons and participants in problem-solving techniques and can be used equally well for training groups of high school students.

Suggest that the students write notes on index cards under subject headings such as "Problem" and "Solution."

2. **Introduce the topic or problem, and state the aim of the discussion.** Explain to the class that a chairperson should introduce the members of the panel if an audience is present and also introduce the topic to the audience.

3. **Allow time for (1) the introduction, (2) the discussion, and (3) a short summary of the conclusions reached.** Suggest that the chairperson lay a watch close by during the discussion as a reminder to stay on schedule. Working out a time schedule before the discussion begins—five minutes to define the problem, for example—is also a good idea.

4. **Keep the discussion orderly.** Explain that a chairperson may or may not require that participants raise their hands or to stand if they wish to speak. In some small groups, discussion may proceed in an orderly way without these constraints.

5. **Give everyone a chance to contribute.** Encourage the chairperson to ask shy participants what they think about the subject. This will insure full participation of the group.

6. **Keep the group's interest at a high pitch.** Suggest that if a chairperson feels that a problem has been thoroughly covered, he or she should suggest moving on to a discussion of solutions. A way to maintain high interest is for the chairperson to play the "devil's advocate" for a few minutes. You may have to explain the meaning of this term to the students: A devil's advocate is a person who assumes a position contrary to that of another person in order to force that person to clarify and defend his or her ideas.

7. **Keep the discussion moving forward.** Remind the students that this is the most difficult of the chairperson's jobs. Often a problem has many facets, which could easily be discussed for hours. It is the duty of the chairperson to monitor the time spent on discussing a problem so that solutions can be considered and conclusions drawn before the time limit is reached.

8. **Take notes on key points made during the discussion.** Suggest that the chairperson, as well as the participants, have small note pads to list important ideas. Emphasize that this is especially important for the chairperson, who must summarize major points.

9. **At the end of the discussion, summarize it briefly.** Stress that the entire discussion, both problems and solutions, should be reviewed.

Your Duties as a Participant

Pages 252–253

Throughout this section, stress the importance of participation to the success of a discussion.

1. **Take part in the discussion.** Make sure that the extroverted and well prepared students allow those who are shy to speak up in the discussion. Remind the students that their ideas, no matter how erratic, probably coincide with those of others in the group or in the audience.

2. **Speak only when the chairperson recognizes you.** Emphasize this important point by explaining that it is impolite to interrupt another participant and that his or her idea may be lost because of interruption.

3. **Speak correctly and distinctly.** You might discuss with students the fact that many rooms are not acoustically sound; therefore, students must project their voices when speaking and when reading supportive material.

4. **Support your statements with facts, examples, or opinions of experts.** Give the group several days to research supporting material. Because the students have studied the use of the library, they should not have great difficulty finding appropriate material.

5. **Keep a sense of direction as the discussion advances.** Explain to the class that if the chairperson falters in his or her job, it is up to the participants to keep the discussion on the right track. Also, note that it is often difficult to restrain one's comments on past topics when the discussion has moved ahead, but it is imperative that this be done.

6. **Listen thoughtfully.** It is quite difficult to listen to participants and think of comments simultaneously. Stress that students must listen to others in order to build upon what they are saying.

7. **Be courteous and tactful.** Most students have a difficult time speaking tactfully to their peers, especially if the participants are their close friends. For this reason, you may decide to assign the students to groups rather than allow them to get together with their friends.

8. **Try to understand the other person's point of view.** Suggest that if students cannot agree on a final solution, they may have to resort to a

compromise decision. Urge them to be amenable to reasonable alternatives and ideas.

Less-Advanced Students. Occasionally appoint these students as the chairpersons of groups that are discussing topics of particular interest to them.

Advanced Students. Encourage these students to polish their skills in leading discussion groups.

A Group Discussion for Analysis

Pages 254–257

You might want to choose eight students to take the roles provided in this model group discussion. Afterwards, use Exercise A on page 257 to analyze the model.

Exercise. Exercise B requires the students to apply the procedures learned in the chapter. If you decide to have the groups hold their discussions in front of the class, the following suggestions may prove to be helpful.

1. The number of participants in each group, excluding the chairperson, should not exceed five people. If there are more, a few of the participants will have difficulty putting forth their ideas.

2. The seating arrangement might be left up to the group with one requirement: that all members should be seen and heard by the audience. If students wish to use a long table, request one in advance of the discussion.

3. Have the groups draw numbers to decide the order of appearance.

4. The groups should decide whether or not to allow questions from the audience. If they decide in favor of this, the questioners should be recognized only by the chairperson. The participants should then provide the answers.

5. Depending upon the topic, the length of the discussion can vary from thirty minutes to the length of the period. If these is time remaining in the period, lead a class analysis of that particular discussion.

6. One way to evaluate a discussion is to ask the audience to list the attributes and the weaknesses of the chairperson and the participants.

Suggest that the audience be somewhat lenient with the first group that speaks, since this is such a new experience for all.

Less-Advanced Students. You may have to assist these students in finding supporting facts, examples, and expert opinions.

Advanced Students. These students may have so much material that two problems might result. The first problem is that time might run out before a solution. The second problem is that these students might monopolize the discussion with a myriad of facts and examples. Warn all students of these two pitfalls and explain that in almost all discussions, some of the material prepared by the participants is not used.

6 Suggestions for Using the HANDBOOK

Any handbook is essentially and primarily a reference book. It is designed for occasional use by someone who seeks information on a particular point of grammar or usage. The most effective handbook is, therefore, one in which material is easy to find, easy to read, full in explanation, and rich in examples. These standards account for the appearance and organization of the Handbook in *Building English Skills*.

Using the Handbook as a Reference Tool

At the beginning of the year it will be profitable to take each class through the Handbook to show its organization and content. The following points should be noted:

1. The Handbook is arranged in 18 numbered sections, each concerned with a different phase of grammar or usage:

   Sections 1–4 provide a thorough treatment of traditional grammar in a contemporary setting.

   Sections 5–9 deal with problems of usage. The students will turn to these sections when they are uncertain as to which form of a word to use.

   Section 10 deals with capitalization. Sections 11–14 deal with problems of punctuation. Sections 15 and 16 give the rules for correct spelling. Section 17 shows correct manuscript form. Section 18 shows how to write an outline.

2. Each numbered entry in the Handbook is a topic, not a rule. Since the topic is usually a short phrase, it is easy to locate. If

there are definitions or general statements of usage (rules), they fall within this section.

3. Within the numbered sections, students should note the full explanation, followed by examples and, where appropriate, by the definition or generalization printed in boldface type. The examples should be studied carefully, for here the students may expect to find a parallel to their own problem. They should be encouraged to read all of the examples within any topic that they are consulting.

4. The wealth of practice sentences provides additional examples in a form that permits students to apply the information they have found. Students should be encouraged to go through a few of these sentences each time they seek and find a particular bit of information.

5. It is especially desirable to take the class through Section 17, on manuscript form, at the beginning of the year to acquaint students with the special helps found here. The most experienced of professional writers find it impossible to keep in mind all of these usages. This section will be highly useful, therefore, as a source of reference for the beginning writer.

Recommended Procedure. Tenth-grade students should be encouraged to use the Handbook on their own. The following procedure will help students figure out where to turn in their Handbooks for the particular help they need.

First, ask under what heading the answer to the problem is likely to be found. If it is a question of grammatical structure or definition, it will be found within the first four sections. If it is a question of parts of speech or verbals, it will be found in Section 1. If it has to do with clauses, it will be found in Section 3. If it concerns the completeness of a sentence, or run-on sentences, it will be found in Section 4. If it concerns any other part of the sentence, it will be found in Section 2.

The Handbook will probably be used by the student most frequently to solve problems of usage, punctuation, capitalization, and manuscript form. The arrangement of Sections 6–17 will help the student find what he or she is looking for. It might be noted that Sections 1 and 2 deal with all verb problems except agreement, which is treated in Section 5, and irregular verbs, which are treated in Section 8.

Using the Handbook for Reteaching and Review

For students with inadequate preparation, the teacher may wish to reteach the elements of grammar and usage. Grouping within the classroom for purposes of drill concerning specific content may sometimes be desirable.

For this kind of reteaching, it is recommended that Sections 1–4 be presented in order. They have been written as a systematic and cumulative study of English grammar. That is, the first section is prerequisite to the second; the second, to the third; etc. In these four sections the explanation is as full as in any lower-grade textbook.

Sections 5–9 which provide a thorough treatment of usage, may also be taught or reviewed systematically. It is recommended, however, that Section 9, which deals primarily with irregular verbs, be used only with classes (or groups within classes) to which these verbs present special difficulties. For other classes or groups, portions of the section may be presented from time to time as needs become evident.

Sections 10–14, dealing with capitalization, punctuation, and spelling, may also be presented systematically. They may be presented in any order that the teacher wishes.

Sections 15 and 16, on spelling, may be taught systematically. The student can then use them for reference.

Finally, all students will profit from a careful study of Sections 17 and 18, Manuscript Form and Outlining, at the beginning of the year.

Individualized Instruction

In all but selected classes, there are sure to be students who do not need extensive teaching. These students may be identified by use of the diagnostic tests included on the following pages of this Manual.

The purpose of these tests is to screen out students who can proceed to use the Handbook independently as need arises. Students who do well on the tests may be given writing assignments or outside reading.

The Diagnostic Tests diagnose the students' skills in the following areas:

Test 1: The Classification of Words
Test 2: The Parts of a Sentence
Test 3: Sentence and Clause
Test 4: Complete Sentences

Test 5: Agreement of Subject and Verb

Test 6: Pronoun Usage

Test 7: Adjective and Adverb Usage

Test 8: Verb Usage

Test 9: The Right Word

Test 10: Capitalization

Test 11: End Marks and Commas

Test 12: The Semicolon, the Colon, the Dash, and Parentheses

Test 13: The Apostrophe

Test 14: Quotations

Test 15: Spelling

Test 16: The Plurals of Nouns

It is suggested that the Diagnostic Tests be given in either of two ways:

1. The tests may be given on three different days, as follows:

First day: Tests 1–4 (Grammar)
Second day: Tests 5–9 (Usage)
Third day: Tests 10–15 (Capitalization, Punctuation, and Spelling)

2. Only a sample testing may be given, as follows:

Test 1: The Classification of Words
Test 2: The Parts of a Sentence
Test 8: Verb Usage
Test 9: Capitalization

In this case, the entire test may be given at one sitting.

Diagnostic Tests

Test 1:   The Classification of Words

Tell the part of speech of the italicized word unless it is a verbal. If it is a verbal, tell whether it is an infinitive, a gerund, or a participle.

1. Every *planet*, including the earth, revolves around the sun. *noun*
2. The tropical forests of *Brazil* are dense and humid. *noun*
3. Dad has a power saw, Bob. *He* will let you use it. *pronoun*
4. *Someone* left his brief case on the bench. *pronoun*
5. W*ho* has seen the movie at Cinema I? *pronoun*
6. The astronomer *spotted* the comet in the southwestern sky. *verb*
7. Jim *felt* his bruised arm tenderly. *verb*
8. A minor *mechanical* defect caused the computer to break down. *adjective*
9. You can see the satellite if you look *hard*. *adverb*
10. The breeze blew *softly* through the aspen leaves. *adverb*
11. Postal rates are probably going up *again*. *adverb*
12. Next year we will have assemblies *during* the fourth period. *prep.*
13. The speaker was bold *but* confused. *conjunction*
14. The problem was hard *to understand*. *infinitive*
15. *Collecting* old comic books is Pat's new hobby. *gerund*

Test 2:   The Parts of the Sentence

Find the verb and the subject.   *subject* ——— *verb* ===

1. People in the stands and players on the field stood in silence.
2. None of us had ever seen or heard of the Herseys.
3. None of the students had ever seen the film before.
4. Bob and his brother were not invited.
5. Here stood the first capitol of the state.
6. Around the bend came the coach with pennants flying.
7. Where in the world has everyone gone?
8. Making a fortune is not my idea of success.
9. All day long, down came the snow.
10. When are the Dawsons coming?

Test 3:   Sentence and Clause

A.   Identify each of the following sentences as either simple, compound, complex, or compound-complex.

1. Jim bought a newspaper and read the want ads. *simple*
2. The superintendent visited our school and spoke at our assembly. *simple*
3. The orchestra and chorus rose and took a bow. *simple*
4. We think of air as weightless, but actually we carry a thousand pounds of it on our shoulders. *compound*
5. If the rain continues, the tennis match will be canceled. *complex*
6. The bus was nearly full, but we piled in. *compound*
7. What the speaker said meant little to us. *complex*
8. You can stay here; however, don't be surprised if you hear strange noises. *compound-complex*
9. Dad stained the cabinet; then he coated it with shellac. *compound*
10. It is now clear that the buses cannot be repaired. *complex*

B.   Identify the following groups of italicized words as either an adjective clause, an adverb clause, or a noun clause.

1. This is the house *where I was born.* *adjective clause*
2. The book *that you asked for* is on reserve. *adjective clause*
3. We left early *because we were tired.* *adverb clause*
4. *When the alarm sounds,* everyone leaves the school. *adverb clause*
5. *Who you are* makes no difference. *noun clause*

Test 4:   Complete Sentences

Two of the following groups of words are sentences. The rest are fragments. Find the fragments and add words needed to make them sentences.

1. The taxi turning around in the middle of the block *fragment*
2. Floods were driving people from their homes *sentence*
3. The crops ruined by water and mud *fragment*
4. Flood control by replanting forests in the mountains *fragment*
5. Because it snowed all day *fragment*
6. The announcement, a warning to all who lived in the village *fragment*
7. Watching the movie, a story of pioneer days in the West *fragment*
8. Some buildings were washed away *sentence*

9. After we had climbed up a long succession of hills *fragment*
10. When rain comes to the desert, a carpet of little flowers *fragment*

Test 5: Agreement of Subject and Verb

Choose the correct word from those given in parentheses.

1. The cost of many of these projects (are, <u>is</u>) too great.
2. We could hardly believe that they (was, <u>were</u>) in earnest.
3. Where (<u>is</u>, are) the delivery of the costumes to be made?
4. (<u>Has</u>, Have) either of the boats been found?
5. Either of those coats (look, <u>looks</u>) good on you.
6. Neither of these mountains (are, <u>is</u>) as high at Mt. McKinley.
7. Each of the rooms (are, <u>is</u>) overcrowded.
8. (Don't, <u>Doesn't</u>) the owner of these lots live around here?
9. The decision of the manager, backed by the directors, (stand, <u>stands</u>).
10. (What's, <u>What are</u>) the plans for the picnic?

Test 6: Pronoun Usage

Choose the correct form from those given in parentheses.

1. How many goals did (<u>he</u>, him) and Chuck make?
2. (<u>They</u>, Them) and the Jeffersons were to blame.
3. Mother gave Chuck and (I, <u>me</u>) a ride to town.
4. (Her, <u>She</u>) and her father have flown to Detroit.
5. It must have been (<u>they</u>, them).
6. (<u>We</u>, Us) two are tuba players in the school band.
7. Between you and (<u>me</u>, I) this lemonade is sour.
8. (<u>We</u>, Us) three have to sing the solo parts.
9. I haven't heard a word from either Judy or (<u>her</u>, she).
10. The Japanese played better volleyball than (<u>we</u>, us).
11. His parents objected to (him, <u>his</u>) reading at the dinner table.
12. Nobody in the audience laughed except (ourselves, <u>us</u>).
13. No one enjoyed the game more than (<u>I</u>, me).
14. Some of the band are wearing (its, <u>their</u>) new uniforms.
15. Neither Edna nor Louise finished (their, <u>her</u>) lunch.

Test 7:   Adjective and Adverb Usage

Choose the correct form from those given in parentheses.

1. The rancher seemed (uneasily, <u>uneasy</u>) about the storm.
2. Dana (quick, <u>quickly</u>) picked up her books and ran to the door.
3. Phil thought he would (certain, <u>certainly</u>) fail the test.
4. The poem sounds (<u>different</u>, differently) in French.
5. You will have (less, <u>fewer</u>) interruptions if you work in the library.
6. You can see just as (good, <u>well</u>) from the balcony.
7. We will sing this part a little more (softer, <u>softly</u>).
8. The farms were hurt (bad, <u>badly</u>) by the hailstorm.
9. The mechanics stayed (steady, <u>steadily</u>) on the job until it was finished.
10. The stores do not sell (these, <u>this</u>) type of stones any more.
11. You can run a small car more (economical, <u>economically</u>) than a large one.
12. We (<u>had</u>, hadn't) barely enough gas to get home.
13. You can't get (them, those, <u>that</u>) kind (no, <u>any</u>) more.
14. There (were, weren't) scarcely any trees left on the farm.
15. We had never seen a (more lovelier, <u>lovelier</u>) day.

Test 8:   Verb Usage

In the sentences below, the present form of the verb is given in parentheses. Substitute either past or past participle, whichever the sentence requires.

1. We had plenty of food but no one had (bring) a can opener. *brought*
2. The driver (swing) the truck off the road. *swung*
3. All day long the sun (shine) hot and bright. *shone*
4. Laura (lend) me her bicycle. *lent*
5. One of our trucks was (catch) in the traffic jam. *caught*
6. By morning the windows were (freeze) shut. *frozen*
7. During the night, two boys had (steal) out of camp. *stolen*
8. The first night we were (bite) by mosquitoes the size of crows. *bitten*
9. She (tear) the wrapping paper off the package. *tore*
10. Helen had never (speak) as cheerfully before about winning the election. *spoken*
11. In the fall, business had (begin) to get better. *begun*

12. Dick (drink) his milk in one gulp and dashed off. *drank*
13. Paul had (sing) so much that he was hoarse. *sung*
14. Have you ever (eat) pineapple ripened in the field? *eaten*
15. Everyone has (go) to the airport to welcome the President. *gone*

Test 9: The Right Word

Choose the correct word from those given in parentheses.

1. My friend Al, who is deaf, (learned, taught) me sign language.
2. Did Margaret Mitchell write other books (besides, beside) *Gone with the Wind?*
3. I know you've done (alot, a lot) of work on this proposal, but I still don't (agree with, agree to) you.
4. Jay said it was (alright, all right) to take the picture without a flashbulb.
5. "You (should have, should of) called for tickets earlier," complained Janet. "There are no good seats left."
6. That magazine article (infers, implies) that all politicians are dishonest.
7. My parents give good (advise, advice), but they (let, leave) me make my own decisions.
8. Argentina and Brazil share a common border, but there are vast differences (among, between) them.
9. This area was (formerly, formally) farm land; now it's a housing development.
10. For a perfect soufflé, carefully fold the egg whites (in, into) the batter.

Test 10: Capitalization

Copy the following sentences, supplying the necessary capital letters.

1. The three states that border on the pacific ocean are california, oregon, and washington.
2. The atlas mountains lie along the northern edge of the african continent.
3. A great many american books have been translated into the japanese language.
4. The number of english-speaking people is growing in the far east.
5. At the head of the great lakes lies the city of duluth.

6. The philadelphia symphony orchestra will play in philharmonic hall.

7. Mark and jill bought a volkswagen bus and traveled through the east during july and august.

8. During our easter vacation, we went to florida and spent two days at walt disney world.

9. The seeds of world war II were planted in the treaty of versailles.

10. Each year thanksgiving day comes on the fourth thursday in november.

Test 11:   End Marks and Commas

A.   Copy these sentences, using end marks and punctuation as required for sentences and abbreviations.

1. Watch out for that truck!

2. Dr. A. C. Bryant will arrive at 1:30 P.M.

3. Mrs. J. C. Kellogg was elected president of the Davis Manufacturing Co., Inc.

4. What historic event took place in 1066 A.D.?

5. The U.S. Post Office at Third Ave. and Fourth St. is to be torn down.

B.   Copy the following sentences, inserting commas where necessary.

1. To get to the station, take the first road to the left.

2. No, we aren't going to the zoo until Saturday.

3. The old car coughed, lurched forward, then shuddered to an obstinate standstill.

4. The speaker, a former astronaut, talked about space flights.

5. Sally, will you please see me after class?

6. Jerry said, however, that he would do the job.

7. Please send the package to 2408 Brandenberry Court, Wheeling, Illinois.

8. The stock market crashed on Thursday, October 24, 1929.

9. From Washington D. C., we flew to Boston, Massachusetts.

10. We searched under the rug, behind the pictures, and in the desk drawers.

Test 12: The Semicolon, the Colon, the Dash, and Parentheses

Copy the following sentences, inserting semicolons, colons, and dashes where necessary.

1. Our opponents were alert;we were not.
2. The prize winners came from Waukegan, Illinois;from Denton, Texas;and from Hillside, New York.
3. The rain began coming down harder;nevertheless, the umpires refused to halt the game.
4. Will the following students please report to the office:Sue, Jack, Betty and Helen.
5. The quotation came from Volume II:pages 65-70.
6. We went down to the‾oh, I wasn't suppose to mention that.
7. The cyclone struck with savage fury;it demolished the little coastal town.
8. Bottles, rags, old tin cans, discarded clothing and papers‾these were his stock in trade.
9. The new traffic control system will be introduced in the following cities:Buffalo, St. Louis, Denver, and Portland.
10. There was a feeling of excitement‾a feeling that now something explosive might occur among the courtroom spectators.

Test 13: The Apostrophe

A. Copy the italicized word, changing it to show ownership or possession correctly.

1. The drop in business is *nobody*‾fault. 's
2. The accident cost me three *week*‾pay. s'
3. The *commander-in-chief*‾flag was flying. 's
4. Where is the *Secretary of the Interior*‾office? 's
5. After a *year*‾wait, Bob got his answer. 's
6. Both *Jackson*‾and *Taylor*‾stores will be open tonight. 's
7. The *Becker*‾and *Irving*‾houses were for sale. 's
8. The *editor-in-chief*‾job is to determine editorial policies. 's
9. The *class*‾decision to sponsor a bike-a-thon was confirmed. 's
10. Bill works at *Bigsby and Roper*‾Store. 's

B. The following sentences contain errors in the use of apostrophes. Copy the sentences, correcting all errors.

1. Harry's and George's exhibit won first prize.
2. Lewis's and Clark's expedition gave the nation a better understanding of it's western territory. *its*
3. We don't know who hit Karen's car.
4. Won't you be staying at your brother's-in-law house? *'s*
5. Robert Frost and Carl Sandburg's poetry readings are available on records. *'s*

Test 14:   Quotations

Copy the following sentences, adding the necessary punctuation marks and capital letters.

1. "Watch that left linebacker," Burt shouted. *"I*
2. "The fire was no accident," the chief retorted. "It was set."
3. "Has everyone been served?" asked Marion.
4. "Do you know," asked Helen, "who won first prize at the Fair?"
5. Billie Jean King wrote an article called "Straight Talk" for *Seventeen* magazine. ·
6. One of my favorite short stories is "An Occurrence at Owl Creek Bridge" by Ambrose Bierce.
7. The officers asked whether we had seen any strangers in the neighborhood.
8. The "quiz," as she called it, turned out to be a full-scale test.
9. We read Carl Sandburg's poem "Chicago" and Poe's "The Raven" in class today.
10. "Are you for us or against us?" Rick demanded.

Test 15:   Spelling

Find the misspelled words in these sentences and spell them correctly.

1. The traffic was moving slowly along the icy road.
2. I do not usually feel lonly when I am alone.
3. The doctor is continuing an intensive x-ray treatment.
4. The guide was very likeable, and his stories were exciting.
5. Mrs. Howard has sent us an invitation to meet a famous artist.
6. The negotiators made a couragous effort to achieve a peaceable settlement.

7. The heav~~y~~ier carriages were almost immov~~e~~able.
8. Nothing succe~~e~~des like success.
9. Natura~~l~~lly, we are willing to concede that the door was locked.
10. The thin~~n~~ess of the paper is rea~~l~~lly an advantage.

Test 16: The Plurals of Nouns

Find the errors in plural forms in the following sentences. Make the necessary corrections.

1. Two of the alto~~s~~s sang solos.
2. The commander~~s~~-in-chief~~s~~ met to plan their strategy.
3. How many cup~~s~~ful~~s~~of flour do you need?
4. How many box~~e~~s of tomatoes did you sell?
5. The thie~~f~~s had broken into the store. *thieves*
6. Several fresh loa~~f~~s of bread were eaten by all the child~~s~~ in the class. *loaves, children*
7. Both of our sister~~s~~-in-law~~s~~ have pianos.
8. The majority~~s~~ in the last election were small. *majorities*
9. You must leave your photo~~s~~s at all the agenc~~y~~s. *agencies*
10. The football coach~~e~~s at our big university are well paid.

7   Keys to Exercises
for
BUILDING ENGLISH SKILLS
Blue Level

Chapter 1

Building Your Vocabulary

(Dictionary definitions for exercises in this chapter are based on *Webster's New World Dictionary of the American Language,* Students Edition.)

Page 4, Exercise A (Definitions may vary somewhat.)

1. before. to plan beforehand
2. outside. very unusual
3. before. to judge beforehand
4. wrong. to judge wrongly
5. within. within the substance of a muscle
6. under or below. under water
7. not. not poisonous
8. outside. beyond the usual function of the senses
9. within. within the veins
10. bad. to fail to function properly
11. good. a blessing
12. wrong. to calculate wrongly
13. not. not violent
14. before. to test beforehand
15. around. to sail or fly around something

Page 4, Exercise B

1. in or into	5. not	9. not
2. not	6. not	10. not
3. in or into	7. in or into	11. not
4. not	8. not	12. not

Page 4, Exercise C

1. illegal	6. transpacific
2. improbable	7. extraterritorial
3. immeasurable	8. misused
4. imflammable	9. nonresidential
5. retell	10. predated

Page 5, Exercise D (Definitions may vary somewhat.)

1. again. to type again
2. across. across the ocean
3. beyond. having a speed greater than the speed of sound
4. the opposite of. to loosen or free
5. in favor of. supporting America
6. the opposite of. to undo or separate; to make clear
7. in favor of. favoring the agreement
8. across. crossing several cultures
9. again. to state again
10. away. to go ashore from a ship
11. very. clever; gifted with genius
12. over and above. having political power over other powerful states
13. not. lacking in patience
14. not. not organic
15. opposite of, not. to treat without due regard

Page 7, Exercise A

1. electrician
2. biologist
3. novelist
4. politician
5. racketeer
6. engineer
7. machinist
8. beautician
9. manager
10. mathematician
11. profiteer
12. idealist

Page 7, Exercise B

1. nonviolence
2. wisdom
3. notice
4. friendliness
5. equality
6. judgment
7. reality
8. assignment
9. addition
10. limitation
11. childhood
12. resignation

Page 9, Exercise A (Definitions will vary somewhat.)

1. inclined to read and study; scholarly
2. careful to avoid danger; wary
3. full of grandeur; impressive
4. keeping awake; alert
5. having the nature of an angel
6. showing or related to addition
7. without equal
8. worthy of praise
9. that can be believed

10. of or connected with plants and animals
11. of or connected with history
12. able to be lessened or put into a simpler form
13. highest in place; foremost
14. giving information readily; talkative
15. triumphant; jubilant

Page 9, Exercise B

Because both the prefix *ir-* and the suffix *-less* convey the meaning "not" or "lacking," the word *irregardless* is redundant. *Regardless* is the correct word.

Page 9, Exercise C

Easily set on fire. Because the prefix *in-* could be construed as "not," *inflammable* could be taken to mean "flameproof." Actually, *inflammable* and *flammable* are synonymous.

Page 9, Exercise D (Dictionary definitions will vary somewhat.)

1. not shortened
2. not practical
3. tending to excite or arouse
4. containing melody; pleasing to hear
5. lack of movement
6. one who translates
7. full of stately display
8. faulty formation of a body or part
9. poorly adjusted
10. tending to prevent something
11. underground
12. lack of adequate ability
13. not giving much knowledge or information
14. vague; not exact
15. the act of conducting; something conducted or completed

Page 11, Exercise A (Definitions may vary somewhat.)

1. take, hold, seize. imprisonment
2. carry. able to be carried
3. believe. belief
4. go, yield, give away. to advance or go on
5. place, put. to place in a certain order

6. speak, say, tell. the act of speaking or reading aloud for someone else to write down
7. do, make. of or pertaining to facts
8. lead. to bring in, introduce
9. go, yield, give away. to be, come, or go before
10. send. to send across
11. do, make. a person who has given help or financial assistance
12. place, put. to change the order or position of
13. believe. believable
14. send. the act of releasing or sending away
15. lead. to teach or inform

Page 11, Exercise B

1. captured	6. receded
2. remit	7. position
3. induction	8. mission
4. factory	9. dictionary
5. credible	10. deposit

Page 12, Exercise A (Definitions may vary somewhat.)

1. look, see. a person who inspects; an official examiner
2. wish. a person who freely offers service; to offer or give of one's own free will
3. write. a writer
4. carry. to carry or send from one country to another
5. stand, put in place. height or size of body
6. turn. to turn upside down
7. carry. a person who carries things
8. see. of or used in television
9. stand, put in place. not moving; at rest
10. carry. carry across
11. call. spoken or sung; oral
12. write. books of the Bible
13. call. to call on; to summon
14. look, see. person who watches an event; onlooker
15. look, see. to have honor or esteem for

Page 12, Exercise B

1. benevolent	5. station
2. vocation	6. spectator
3. reverted	7. invisible
4. imported	8. spectacles

Page 14, Exercise A

1. capt—take, hold seize
2. cred—believe
3. mit—send
4. spec—look
5. vis—see
6. port—carry
7. pon, pos, posit—place, put
8. cede, cess—yield, give away
9. duc, duct—lead

Page 14, Exercise B (Definitions may vary somewhat.)

2. dictator—dic, dict—speak, say, tell—person whose word must be obeyed
3. reverse—vers, vert—turn—to turn backward
4. circumspect—spec—look, see—cautious, careful
5. vocal—voc, vok—call—spoken or sung, oral
6. benefactor—fac, fec—do, make—one who gives help or financial assistance
7. malevolent—vol—wish—to wish harm to others
8. substation—stat—stand, put in place—a branch station

Page 14, Exercise C (Student versions of the paragraphs will vary.)

Although I do not choose to do so, I must put upon my otherwise kindly face a mood and tone of severity and impatience. You have been told many times about my unusually broad knowledge of non-earthly beings. Also, I have frequently guessed about the bad effects of travel between planets by those who live in alien galaxies. Uppermost in my concerns are the distasteful Green Pooklas from the planet Gerbigen. Paying no attention to my informative speeches and thought-provoking lectures as your chairperson, those determined invaders have been allowed to unload their highly unusual space vehicles in suburban Zonar. Their occupation of the Stellar Pad has greatly distressed the Zonar Startreks. I am certain that the situation is threatening.

Legislation, namely a law discouraging association with such horrible individuals as the Green Pooklas, must be introduced immediately. My more lenient opponents must be talked out of their uncertain position. Do not allow them to avoid the issue. The law must be unchangeable and clear. The evil Green Pooklas, superhuman though they may appear, are disruptive and bent on invasion. The dauntless Zonar Startreks must regain their working place. And as fair, unbiased realists, we must find another site for future Pookla teams seeking a place to camp. However, Zonar must be made safe from further non-earthly interference.

Chapter 2
Using the Dictionary To Build Word Power

(Definitions and word derivations for exercises in this chapter are based on *Webster's New World Dictionary of the American Language*, Student Edition.)

Page 21, Exercise

1. the tracing of a word back to its origins
2. under *tailor*
3. under *insignia*
4. a listing or discussion of words having similar meanings
5. under *follow*
6. vt. example: The local hospital tries to enlist students to work as volunteers.

   vi. example: Many graduating seniors enlist in the Army to learn a trade.
7. a foreign phrase. These foreign words have been incorporated into the English vocabulary because of wide usage.
8. an Americanism
9. derived from
10. that the entry word is a suffix

Page 25, Exercise C (Answers will vary somewhat.)

1. to go quietly or secretly
2. to get loose from
3. to escape
4. a small piece of paper
5. a pillowcase
6. to slide accidentally
7. a space between piers for docking
8. a young, slim person
9. a stem or root cut for planting
10. to put or move smoothly
11. to let loose to follow game
12. an error

Page 26, Exercise D (Definitions may vary slightly.)

1. went over quickly but thoroughly
2. a group following the same teachings or methods
3. the main area for shelving books in a library
4. readily convertible into cash
5. a tilting or inclining to one side

Page 30, Exercise B (Answers will vary somewhat.)

1. imprecise, reckless
2. lasting, permanent
3. obscure, unknown
4. cruel, brutal, unkind
5. expensive, costly
6. stop, cease
7. provincial, unsophisticated
8. postscript, epilog, finale
9. fireproof, flameproof
10. hopeful, elated

Page 30, Exercise A

1. *Agriculture* is derived from the Latin words *ager,* meaning "field," and *cultura,* meaning "cultivation."
2. *Belligerent* comes from the Latin word *bellum,* meaning "war," from which we also get *duel.*
3. The word *carnival* translates from Latin as "removal of meat," from *carne,* meaning "flesh." The carnival in the traditional Christian calendar is a period of feasting and merrymaking immediately preceding Lent, so the word refers to abstinence from meat during the forty days of Lent.
4. *Corduroy* comes from the French words *cord du roi,* meaning "king's cord."
5. *Curfew* is based on the French and Latin words for "to cover" and "fireplace." In the Middle Ages a bell every evening signalled the time to cover fires and retire for the night.
6. *Czar* originated as the Russian name for Caesar, the Roman statesman and general.
7. *Delta* comes from the letter of the Greek alphabet, delta, which is triangular in shape.
8. *Intoxicate* comes from the Latin *intoxicare,* "to drug or poison," which is derived from the Greek word, *toxicon,* for the poison in which poison arrows were dipped.
9. *Landau* comes from the name of the German town, Landau, in which the original landau carriage was made.
10. *League* is derived from the Latin word *ligare,* meaning "to bind." *League* as a measure of distance has been used since ancient times, and the Gauls made it equal 1,500 Roman paces (2.2 km.).
11. *Lieutenant* evolved from the Middle French words for "holding" and "place" to signify the holding of a certain rank.
12. *Mob* is short for *mobile,* which is the Latin word for "the changeable crowd, the movable common people."
13. *Nausea* is derived from the Greek word *nausia,* for "seasickness." It evolved from *naus,* meaning "ship," from which we also get *nave* and *nautical.*
14. *Ogle* probably comes from the Low German word for "eye."

15. *Emancipate* literally means "to take away hand"; it comes from the Latin *e-*, meaning "away," combined with *manus* for "hand" and *capere* for "take." Ironically, under Roman law *emancipate* meant "to enslave, to deliver into bondage."
16. *Guerrilla* literally means "small war" in Spanish as the diminutive of *guerra*, "war." The first modern guerrilla operation on a large scale was in Spain in 1808–13, when *guerrilla* was coined to describe independent action by the remnants of the Spanish army against the French occupiers.
17. *Gymnasium* is the Latin word for "school" from the Greek *gymnasion*, meaning "to train naked," which comes from *gymnos*, "naked." In ancient Greece a gymnasion was an area for physical exercise, which was done in the nude. In time, the gymnasion became an institution of learning in Greece, and in the Renaissance the term resurfaced as the name of a classical school. The modern gymnasium began in Germany, where gyms were essential at secondary schools.
18. *Pedigree* is derived from the Middle French *pei de grue*, which translates "crane's foot." It refers to the appearance of the lines in a genealogical tree.
19. *Sinecure* evolved from the Latin words *sine cura*, meaning "without care of souls," to designate a paid church office not involving spiritual care. It has come to mean "an office that requires little or no work and provides an income."
20. *Tenor* is adapted from the word *tenere*, meaning "to hold" in Latin, because the tenor voice held the melody.

Page 31, Exercise B

1. *Dexter* is the Latin word for "right."
2. *Á droit* are the French words meaning "to the right."
3. The French word for "left" *gauche* comes from the Middle French *gauchir*, "to become warped."
4. *Sinister* is derived from the Latin word meaning "left-hand or unlucky side." Right-handedness has always been associated with power and justice, left-handedness with weakness and evil.

Page 31, Exercise

Following are the names associated with each word.

1. *cereal:* Ceres, the Roman goddess of agriculture
2. *chauvinist:* N. Chauvin, a fanatically patriotic Napoleonic soldier
3. *galvanize:* Luigi Galvani, Italian physicist

4. *gerrymander:* E. Gerry, the governor of Massachusetts when gerrymandering was employed
5. *guillotine:* J. I. Guillotin, who advocated the use of the guillotine
6. *leotard:* J. Léotard, a 19th century French aerialist
7. *mesmerize:* F. A. Mesmer, a German physician
8. *pantaloon:* Pantalone, the Venetian patron saint
9. *pasteurize:* L. Pasteur, a French bacteriologist
10. *quixotic:* Don Quixote, Cervantes' romantic hero
11. *sandwich:* 4th Earl of Sandwich. It is said that he ate sandwiches while gambling so that he would not need to leave for meals.
12. *saxophone:* A. J. Sax, a Belgian inventor
13. *lynch:* Capt. William Lynch, an 18th century Virginia vigilante
14. *macadam:* J. L. McAdam, a Scottish engineer
15. *martial:* Mars, the Roman war god
16. *maudlin:* Mary Magdalene, who is often represented as weeping
17. *maverick:* S. Maverick, a 19th century Texas rancher who did not brand his cattle
18. *mercurial:* Mercury, the Roman messenger god
19. *sequoia:* Sequoya, an American Indian who worked out the Cherokees' written symbols for their language
20. *shrapnel:* H. Shrapnel, the British general who invented shrapnel
21. *sideburns:* A. E. Burnside, a Union general in the Civil War
22. *teddy bear:* Theodore Roosevelt, the 26th U.S. President
23. *vulcanize:* Vulcan, the Roman god of fire and metalworking
24. *watt:* James Watt, a Scottish engineer and inventor

Chapter 3
Combining Ideas in Sentences

Page 35, Exercise A

1. Will Tom be able to rejoin the team, or will he have to sit out the whole season?
2. I remembered the eggs, but I forgot the butter.
3. Jane sanded the tabletop, and Phil assembled the base.
4. Would help arrive in time, or would we be stranded on the mountaintop all night?
5. Rain began to fall in torrents, and the players sprinted for the shelter of the dugout.
6. Lucille is not as fast as Joan, but she has more endurance.
7. Pine is much less expensive than oak, but it is not as sturdy.
8. My parents are on a business trip, and I'm staying with Jeff's family.
9. Shall I eat all this tomato soup, or would you like some?
10. The tax bill passed easily, but the leash law was defeated by a wide margin.

Page 35, Exercise B

1. Jenny thought that she had finished the test, but she had overlooked the last problem.
2. Chris ran after the bus, but she was not able to catch it.
3. Add the cubed potatoes, and then simmer the soup for an hour.
4. You can walk from Knox Street to Third Avenue, or you can take the crosstown bus.
5. Motorcycles are economical, but a car offers better protection from the weather.

Page 36, Exercise A

1. We will take the train or the bus to El Paso.
2. We led for most of the game but lost in the final seconds.
3. Phil did not want to go at first but changed his mind at the last minute.
4. Success may come overnight or after years of struggling.
5. I'd like to go to Denver and San Francisco.
6. We have plenty of asparagus but no broccoli.
7. I stopped at Dan's house and asked him to come to dinner.

8. Parker could inch his way along the narrow ledge or risk everything in a leap across the chasm.
9. The brown bear rolled over in the sun and yawned.
10. Wash the cut with disinfectant and bandage it carefully to prevent infection.

Page 37, Exercise B

1. I want to become a biologist or a Grand National Stock Car driver. (The use of *and* is also acceptable.)
2. I bought my mother some flowers and took her out to dinner.
3. John was here this morning but left before noon.
4. The shopping cart rolled down the hill and into the oncoming traffic.
5. I ran well at the start but dropped out after the first hill.

Page 38, Exercise A

1. Susan had a severe cold.
2. John returned all the overdue books.
3. Detective Bass studied the broken window.
4. A whimpering boy stood in the aisle.
5. The completed reports are in that pile.
6. Ethel took the whistling tea kettle from the stove.
7. The silence was shattered by a howling wolf.
8. A circling buzzard glided toward the ground.
9. A spotted dog has been following me to school every day for a week.
10. Mrs. Walker spoke of her treasured childhood memories.

Page 38, Exercise B

1. We had some of Jon's delicious lasagna for dinner.
2. Officer Page caught the speeding car at the light.
3. Jane walked along the deserted street.
4. This cracked glass should be thrown out.
5. A sleeping cat was curled up in a spot of sun.

Page 39, Exercise A

1. At the end of the film, a huge snake crushed several tall buildings.
2. Frank threw a low, outside pitch to Becky.
3. Becky hit a sizzling line drive right at Jeff on third.

4. The crafty old fox circled the chicken coop.
5. A thin slice of fiery red sun peeked over the horizon.
6. In the dim light I could just make out a weathered face.
7. We reached the summit after a long and exhausting climb.
8. Thin strips of zesty orange peel add unusual flavor to a stew.
9. John gave a long, low, heartfelt sigh of relief.
10. The next scheduled meet will be held in Westlake's heated pool.

Page 40, Exercise B

1. Dan found a crumpled old letter in a dusty book on the top shelf.
2. The mysterious stranger stood alone in the still, damp night.
3. The commuters enjoyed their swift, comfortable ride on the new lightweight cars.
4. The laughing, whooping cry of the loon is unmistakable.
5. I'll have fried eggs and chilled tomato juice.

Page 41, Exercise (Sentences may vary somewhat.)

1. Kurt smiled strangely at me.
2. Jim secretly dreamed of playing shortstop for the Yankees.
3. Detective Bass closely inspected the fingerprints.
4. Diana talked endlessly about her mountain-climbing adventures.
5. Mr. Swanson had parked illegally on the bridge.

Page 43, Exercise A (Sentences may vary somewhat.)

1. Mr. Perkins was waiting in the lobby.
2. A tall woman carrying a briefcase stood on the corner.
3. Opening the envelope, I found three pages from my laboratory report.
4. Dazzled by the beauty of the falls, we watched without moving.
5. After the storm, a brilliant rainbow arched across the sky.
6. Katy spent every summer in the country with her grandmother.
7. After the game, John Layne, our starting quarterback, praised the opposition.
8. My first class each morning was biology, my favorite subject.
9. Diana, a short girl playing in her first full season, was chosen for the all-star team.
10. The downtown area, destroyed by fire in 1882, was entirely reconstructed by 1884.

Page 43, Exercise B (Sentences may vary somewhat.)

1. Standing alone beneath a streetlamp, Cliff had no idea that he was being watched.
2. We had been reading *I Am Third*, the autobiography of Gale Sayers.
3. Archeologists flocked to the site of the ancient city discovered by Professor Greene and her students.
4. After dinner, Dr. Watson settled back and began a story about one of Holmes's famous cases.
5. Concentrating fiercely on her paper, Rosa did not hear the telephone in the next room.

Page 44, Exercise A

1. Working at an after-school job kept Renee from joining the track team.
2. Refusing to pay his debts led Phillip into serious trouble.
3. Visiting the statewide science fair was the beginning of Martha's interest in science.
4. Getting a good night's sleep before a test is a much better idea than cramming until late at night.
5. Recycling paper saves forests, energy, and money.
6. Booing when the other team took the court was a mistake that we later regretted.
7. Competing in the city marathon climaxed Mrs. Benson's fitness program.
8. They enjoyed discussing politics and world affairs at dinner.
9. We hope that holding our meetings in the evening will increase attendance.
10. Listening to a record can never take the place of seeing a live performance.

Page 45, Exercise B

1. Missing the last bus home meant that Maria would be at least an hour late.
2. Climbing the Matterhorn at sixty years of age brought Mr. Daniels his greatest thrill.
3. Having to rest in bed after an illness can be depressing for an active person.
4. Discovering Parkinson's true identity enabled me to solve the mystery.
5. Slipping as he rounded the final turn cost Cliff first place.

Page 45, Review Exercise A

1. Would you like to borrow my pen, or do you prefer to use a pencil?
2. The birds haven't discovered the feeder, but the squirrels have.
3. I made that feeder myself, and then I mounted it on a tall pole.
4. Would a taller pole discourage the squirrels, or will I just have to put up with them?
5. Time was running out, and I still had three questions to answer.

Page 46, Exercise B

1. You might make the table with ash or birch.
2. They peered through the window but couldn't see anyone inside.
3. Glen asked several questions but still wasn't certain that he understood the problem.
4. We can meet today at noon or tomorrow at three.
5. I have relatives living in St. Louis and Oakland.

Page 46, Exercise C

1. A frigid wind blew from the mountains.
2. I had just begun my first job.
3. Detective Bass questioned the nervous witness.
4. This project could not have been completed without the help of many tireless people.
5. Sunlight glittered on the frosted windowpanes.

Page 46, Exercise D

1. Early that morning, a mysterious message arrived from the missing crew members.
2. Parker gave a calm, thoughtful speech.
3. Could my trembling voice be heard over the screaming crowd?
4. I started the day with a plate of fluffy scrambled eggs.
5. A large, shaggy, gray dog loped along beside me as I ran.

Page 47, Exercise E (Sentences may vary somewhat.)

1. Ann stepped carefully into the center of the mat.
2. Carl frequently visited the patients in the children's wing of the hospital.
3. Detective Bass questioned every suspect extensively.

4. Marsha wandered aimlessly through the park.
5. Mr. Johnson was attempting frantically to get our attention.

Page 47, Exercise F (Sentences may vary somewhat.)

1. Mrs. Daniels was standing at the side of the stage.
2. A trio of music students playing violins wandered through the park.
3. Turning the corner, I ran into two people from my old neighborhood.
4. Stunned by the ending of the film, we sat motionless in our seats.
5. After the victory parade, confetti littered Main Street.

Page 47, Exercise G

1. Finishing my history paper gave me a real sense of accomplishment.
2. Refinishing old furniture has brought the Andersons a second income.
3. Explaining her position in a calm and logical way won Lucille the respect of everyone in the audience.
4. Bragging has cost Bill many friends.
5. Planning ahead can prevent wasted time and effort.

Chapter 4
Improving Your Sentences

Page 51, Exercise A (Revised sentences may vary somewhat.)

1. Ceramics is an interesting hobby because it combines manual skill with artistic imagination.
2. Learning a new language is difficult because entirely new vocabulary, grammar, pronunciation, and idioms must be mastered.
3. I have always wanted to be on a basketball team because I like the strenuous excitement of the game.
4. During those few days I began to admire his fine character, specifically, his honesty and generosity.
5. Mike chose the book he was reading for three good reasons: its action-packed plot, its true-to-life characters, and its humorous style.
6. With fine workmanship for a low price, the $75 Yamaha is a good guitar for a beginner.
7. The fight was foolish since it did not resolve our disagreement.
8. The hero was a typical middle-aged American. He worked hard, lived comfortably, and mowed his lawn every Saturday.
9. I liked the Robert Redford movie because the suspense built to a thrilling finish.
10. My sister Fran is always joking. Her specialties are teasing my brother and pulling tricks on my Dad.

Page 51, Exercise B (Revised sentences may vary somewhat.)

1. I'd like to be a lifeguard because even without pay I enjoy swimming, sunning, and ogling people.
2. I flunked the test because I hadn't studied.
3. Stereo speakers should be at least ten feet apart to ensure full amplification of the sound.
4. Because many people are tired of rock music, Scott Joplin's ragtime has become a nostalgic favorite.
5. More women are running for government office as a result of the women's rights movement and the widespread cynicism about established politicians.
6. Inflation has become a huge problem because many people's salaries are not keeping pace with higher costs.
7. In order to arouse interest I will reveal most of the story's plot, but not the ending.
8. I prefer to be with my friends because they have more fun than the other people I know.

9. My freshman year was a good one because I liked my courses and did well in them.
10. I liked the waltzing bear because of the silly contrast between his gigantic size and his delicate dance.

Page 54, Exercise A (Revised sentences may vary.)

1. The unpleasantness started when Sue refused the invitation.
2. Agnes decided on a green dress because she has red hair.
3. He thought I owed the teacher an apology.
4. The number of accidents caused by sheer carelessness on our highways is staggering.
5. I did not like to retrace my steps on the deserted street.
6. Jo thought that if she acted quickly, she could get the job.
7. Since I have reached the ripe old age of sixteen, I hope to get a job this summer.
8. The salesman explained that we did not have to pay the total cost in order to have the bicycle delivered.
9. Mike wanted to lose a few pounds because his favorite slacks did not fit him.
10. The class prepared a program dedicated to Mozart, a great musician.

Page 55, Exercise B (Revised sentences may vary.)

1. It started with fighting in the streets.
2. During the Vietnam War people's attitudes changed drastically.
3. It is time for a great leader like Abraham Lincoln or Franklin D. Roosevelt.
4. Deaf people usually are safe drivers because they are aware of their handicap.
5. Because our house has been sold, we will be moving soon.
6. My weight bothers me.
7. Because Dad did not have any gray paint, he used brown to paint the steps.
8. I don't like shirts without pockets.
9. We were late because we missed the plane.
10. I saw a suspicious-looking woman slip into the telephone booth.

Page 58, Exercise A (Revised sentences may vary somewhat.)

1. At the museum's science fair, Jack Gorman's robot caused a great deal of excitement. People came from miles around to watch Jack demonstrate it.

2. Scientists say that foods eaten as quickly as possible after picking contain essential vitamins. They also say that foods lose vitamins with prolonged cooking.
3. A teen-age girl may panic about going out with a boy she has never dated unless she knows what to wear, how to be attractive, and what to say.
4. Mathematics trains people to think straight and solve problems.
5. Because baseball was not popular in 1900, there weren't many good players. However, he enjoyed baseball and played it well.

Page 58, Exercise B (Revised sentences may vary somewhat.)

1. The owners realize that we will annoy them for only three months. When we return to school in September, our summer fun will be only a pleasant dream.
2. I liked the movie better than the book because the movie made the characters seem more real than the book did.
3. While I cover various stories, I will learn new information and better understand familiar situations. I will also help readers to comprehend world events.
4. She didn't ask to walk home with me. I was walking alone, thinking of my first unhappy day of school and of the dreary days ahead, when a friendly voice called, "Hi! I'm Patsy Walker."
5. Sleep is fascinating to me. During sleep I dream of places that are familiar, special, or even imaginary.

Page 59, Exercise C (Revised sentences may vary somewhat.)

1. I want to be a deep-sea diver because I enjoy the thrill of learning about undersea life.
2. In *All the President's Men,* a movie about Watergate, Robert Redford and Dustin Hoffman play the two reporters who investigated and exposed the Watergate break-in.
3. I believe some kinds of criticism are good while other kinds are harmful. Harmful criticism degrades rather than helps a person.
4. English setters are a rare breed. When we walk our two, Melissa and Storm, people ask what kind of dogs they are.
5. Billy the Kid, America's best-known outlaw, had an innocent baby-faced look. He never used his real name, Henry McCarthy.

Page 60, Exercise A (Revised sentences may vary somewhat.)

1. Harold's older brother is completely different from Harold in appearance and interests.

2. The school band was invited to play at a band competition in Washington, D.C.
3. Supersonic passenger planes have made great changes in the way people travel around the world.
4. The all-girl rock group toured the state all summer.
5. The book I am reading contains information about the most recent developments in the field of electronics.
6. Many of my friends are fond of bowling.
7. Last Saturday I saw a basketball game that went into double overtime.
8. At Grandmother's house, a table was prepared on which there was an abundance of bread, butter, cake, colored eggs, ham, chicken, and other food.
9. The play was about two soldiers who became friends during World War II and who were reunited years later.
10. I want to work in television or radio because the audience will be doubled in ten years and more technicians will be in demand.

Page 61, Exercise B (Revised sentences may vary somewhat.)

1. After I die, I want to be remembered for what I accomplished.
2. I used to live with my parents in suburban Woodland Hills. Now I live with my mother in Los Angeles, which is called "the city of angels" in spite of my presence.
3. Only after Uncle Dan's death last year did I realize what a wonderful friend he had been.
4. With only one clue, a piece of cord from a Venetian blind, the police began interviewing all cord wholesalers in Miami.
5. Chicago, which has been called "the city that works," was run by Richard J. Daley, who had been the mayor for twenty years. He died suddenly while in office in December, 1976.

Page 62, Exercise A (Revised sentences may vary somewhat.)

1. No matter how much we reasoned with him, the coach wouldn't put Jack back in the game.
2. The crippled plane circled the field for three hours to use up most of its fuel before landing.
3. If we had worked together, we could have won the state championship last year.
4. If I had an interest in chemistry, I could learn the subject more thoroughly
5. College graduates receive higher salaries on account of their additional training and knowledge.

6. Because I was in town, I decided to buy my parents their Christmas presents.
7. Are there people on other planets who are discovering important facts about the earth by methods that we do not know?
8. My parents are renting a bungalow at the shore for the whole month of August.
9. Although my friends would not believe it, I have two medals for diving.
10. Since there was neither television nor radio at the time, the gleeman reported news of current happenings to the people.

Page 63, Exercise B (Revised sentences may vary somewhat.)

1. This 1924 airmail stamp is worth $400, I am told.
2. Throughout history there have been only seven basic jokes.
3. In spite of what many think, wolves never attack people.
4. The Hawaiian Islands were discovered by Captain James Cook in 1778.
5. The coach announced right after the game that she had resigned.
6. Until he got his new Leica, most of Sam's snapshots had a washed-out look.
7. Frankly, my bicycle and I are no longer friends.
8. Even though it was a late-model car, it had a suspiciously low price.
9. Keeping up with progress, many offices have electric pencil sharpeners.
10. According to a psychologist, people who wear bow ties are not very trustworthy.

Page 66, Exercise A (Revised sentences may vary somewhat.)

1. The noisy plane that zoomed overhead was a 747 flying nonstop to California.
2. Because the game went into overtime, the coach was too late in leaving school to appear for his broadcast at the local studio.
3. I love to watch the snow start its long journey from the sky to the ground. There the snowflakes lie in all shapes until people finally step on them or shovel them away.
4. As he was watching a television play, he decided that it was the worst he had ever seen. He was so disappointed in the program that he turned it off.
5. The bugle corps lined up for the precision drill and maneuvers. After an award-winning performance, they carried the trophy home in triumph.

6. The train pulled out of the station, gradually picking up speed. Jim picked up his suitcase and went home, disappointed that his journey was over.
7. Because the girl who had the leading role in the school play got the measles, I was given the part. I had only three days to rehearse for the performance.
8. The audience filed into their places for the first performance of the school show. Because a record crowd turned out, the total box-office receipts were very high.
9. When my sister was born, I felt that my mother and father didn't love me any more. My mother sensed my insecurity and assured me she loved all of us equally.
10. On the way home from the beach the traffic was very light. The day of surf and sand had left us all with bad sunburns.

Page 67, Exercise B (Answers may vary somewhat.)

1. however
2. on the other hand
3. instead, consequently
4. nonetheless
5. furthermore
6. however
7. nevertheless
8. therefore
9. hence, thus
10. besides
11. still
12. however
13. or
14. otherwise
15. however

Page 70, Exercise A (Revised sentences may vary somewhat.)

1. After listening to my father's advice, I decided to take chemistry.
2. Edna Sloan, our best runner, won the cross-country race.
3. Although I had taken every precaution, the pictures did not turn out well.
4. Though he had great obstacles to overcome, Mark Twain became a very popular writer.
5. My older sister bought a new car, a 1980 Pinto.
6. Because we won the league games for three successive years, we have permanent possession of the trophy.
7. Because I had prepared my lesson thoroughly the night before, I wasn't worried about the test.
8. Dolores had decided on a career in marine biology.
9. Although all preparations were made carefully, the rocket exploded.
10. Since bacteria build up immunity to certain antibiotics, new drugs have to be produced.

11. Although our school has many brilliant students, we did not get a National Merit Scholarship.
12. Listening to his new stereo recordings, Don did not notice how late it was.
13. Though Fred kept looking, he still couldn't find the ball.
14. I sometimes think about death, which happens to everyone.
15. Mr. Novak told me to interview Miss Carnahan, the personnel manager at the Sara Lee plant.

Page 71, Exercise B (Revised sentences may vary slightly.)

1. Not being able to read the directions, she could not knit the sweater.
2. Although Joan is the top-ranking student in her class, she is not going to college.
3. As I was walking down the street yesterday, I met a friend I hadn't seen in years.
4. Seeing his little brother in tears, Ted hurried to help him.
5. Although there was to be an important meeting of the student officers after school, the president left at the regular time.
6. Because wolves are rare, they are on the endangered species list.
7. When I stepped off the plane at Kennedy Airport, I noticed a crowd waiting behind the fence.
8. Because Dad was busy with his monthly report, he hardly heard a word I said.
9. Grabbing a sandwich from the tray, she dashed out of the house.
10. People who really value privacy don't like this neighborhood.

Page 73, Exercise A (Revised sentences will vary somewhat.)

1. Dad visited the towns where he was born and where he grew up.
2. At last I came to a road I knew that led home.
3. When you first meet him, you consider him to be a little odd and sickly.
4. We are going on a trip to Atlantic City, a popular resort.
5. High school chemistry teaches about distilling water and analyzing compounds.
6. This course teaches accuracy and speed.
7. Everyone wants to avoid accidents and illnesses.
8. Our neighbors, the Deckers, won a trip to Mexico last month.
9. Jo had to choose between taking singing lessons and learning ballet.
10. My brother wanted a trip around the world and a ride in a supersonic plane.

Page 73, Exercise B (Revised sentences will vary somewhat.)

1. She has many accomplishments: horseback riding, dancing, skin-diving, and swimming.
2. We decided to investigate further, hoping to find clues in the locked room.
3. The coach was a man of experience and patience.
4. My brother has a job gassing up cars, picking up trash, and running errands.
5. The woman was old, sick, and toothless.
6. Gloria Steinem did not want a job taking dictation or doing filing.
7. Following the trail is easier than cutting through the woods.
8. The salad dressing splattered on the table, on the rug, and on Mr. Grimly's suit.
9. The typical American changes jobs seven times and careers three times.
10. Laura is a good babysitter and a reliable person.

Page 74, Review Exercise A (Revised sentences may vary somewhat.)

1. I think the leather jackets in the basement are better buys than the ones on the main floor.
2. Although the roads were terrible and the car ride was bumpy, we enjoyed the trip.
3. I like to watch professional tennis because the action is fast-paced and the competition is keen.
4. I haven't learned how to program a computer yet.
5. We were fortunate to have a spare tire.
6. The mayor herself cut the cake.
7. I must admit that I bungled the job.
8. Dad was shocked by the size of the dinner check.
9. The stand-up comedian, who was the last person on the show, was a very funny fellow.
10. When the electrician touched a live wire, she was electrocuted.

Page 74, Review Exercise B (Revised sentences may vary somewhat.)

1. Hank Aaron hit 733 home runs in his career, more than any other baseball player.
2. Because I was startled by Selma's remark, I just sat there and said nothing.

3. In spite of the long waits in line, our trip to Disney World was fun for every member of the family.
4. When my brother Jack came home from college, he said his grades were so low he needed a snorkel. Because he always gets good grades, I knew he was only joking.
5. My grandmother is a successful accountant, a professional clarinetist, and a devoted dog breeder.
6. After finding two matching wedding bands in McDonald's driveway, Dad put a notice in the paper.
7. When I was only three years old, my family moved from Boston to Louisville. We have lived there ever since.
8. The Queen of England was trained as a mechanic during World War II.
9. On the way to the theater our fuel pump broke. While we waited for our car to be towed away and repaired, we missed the first act of the play.
10. Scientists have landed some equipment, including a seismometer, on Mars. They plan to investigate Martian earthquakes, called "Marsquakes."

Chapter 6
Writing Effective Paragraphs

Page 90, Exercise (These are sample revisions. Acceptable paragraphs will vary.)

1. This is a well organized paragraph that describes the entrapment, devastation, and death caused by a storm.
2. This is a well organized paragraph that describes the first moments of a parachute jump.
3. This paragraph lacks unity because it combines two unrelated ideas: Native American farming methods and Native American place names. The first or the second sentence could function as the topic sentence, although the development of the second sentence would require additional information.

   Native Americans have contributed a great deal to American farming methods. The white settlers in Colonial America might have starved if they had not copied Indian methods. The Indians had developed effective planting and harvesting techniques; and at least one tribe, the Pima, had a well developed irrigation system.
4. This is a well organized paragraph that focuses on a woman's feelings and actions the morning after a fire has destroyed her home.
5. The unity of this paragraph is violated by two sentences, one that differentiates between the geographic and magnetic North Poles and one that notes the arrival of the Nautilus and the Skate at the North Pole.

   About five in the afternoon we submerged and set our course for the North Pole. All through the night, as we sped northward, the ice detector and television scanned the surface in vain for patches of thin ice. Our belief that we would find thin ice frequently enough to surface at will began to seem overly optimistic. Our plan to surface precisely at the North Pole began to look hopeless.
6. This paragraph contains three sentences that do not add to the description of the scene. Also, the first sentence establishes a pleasant mood, which conflicts with the somberness of the other images.

   On a dull, cloud day I stood looking down a dirty street. Nearby was a weathered old tenement house. The paint had peeled from the walls, and what had once been a front porch was now a mass of splintered, rotted wood. In the shadows a little girl stood holding a doll with a broken head in her arms. She was crying.
7. All the sentences in this paragraph describe one place: a country road.

8. This is a well organized paragraph about the examination of a bat and a girl's thoughts about the creature.
9. This entire paragraph is an attempt to characterize the Mexican people; it is a well organized, unified paragraph that develops this single idea.
10. This paragraph requires extensive revision and is, therefore, the most difficult of those in the exercise. A student might choose to write a topic sentence about what ways of walking can reveal about people, about the baggage claim area as a place to observe a wide range of emotional states, or about the observations made during one specific trip to and from a baggage claim area. The development of each idea requires the retention and modification of different sentences and the addition of different kinds of information.

Page 96, Exercise

1. This paragraph does not keep the contract implied in the topic sentence, but rather, introduces several different ideas about Kitty O'Neil: her interest in handicapped children, her diet, her proficiency as a stuntwoman. To create a unified, well developed paragraph, a writer might build on the first two sentences in the paragraph, adding several examples of the achievements that led to her title "fastest woman alive."
2. This paragraph keeps the contract implied in the topic sentence. It cites several examples of a puzzling natural phenomenon.
3. This paragraph does not keep its contract. Although the topic sentence introduces the idea of sky diving, the rest of the paragraph deals with a swimming theme. The paragraph could be revised by deleting the sentence about sky diving, thus turning the second sentence into the topic sentence of the revised paragraph.
4. The writer of this paragraph does not keep his contract because the details of the paragraph are not consistent with the key word *terrifying*. Words such as *comforting, softly,* and *familiarly* create the opposite impression. To revise this paragraph, a writer might write a new topic sentence such as this: I settled down for a quiet evening at home.
5. This paragraph keeps its contract by describing the incident signaled by the barking dog.
6. The writer of this paragraph describes a scene in which a moose is the central figure. Because the focus of the paragraph is the entire scene, not only the moose, the sentence about the water hens and the crested grebe is directly related to the main idea of the paragraph. The writer has kept her contract with her readers.
7. This paragraph does not keep the contract because the idea in the topic sentence is not explained by the supporting sentences. In fact, the second and third sentences introduce new ideas: exceptions to

weird diets and the necessity of selecting from the four food groups. To revise this paragraph, a writer might delete the second and third sentences, then add several sentences that describe strange diets.

8. This writer adheres strictly to the contract stated in the topic sentence. Specific facts support the summarizing first sentence about reports of the yeti.

Page 102, Exercise A

1. b   3. a   5. a   7. b   9. a
2. a   4. b   6. a   8. b   10. b

Page 103, Exercise B

1. b   3. a   5. a   7. b   9. b
2. a   4. b   6. b   8. a   10. a

Page 104, Exercise C (These are sample sentences. Acceptable responses will vary.)

1. Bamboo, a type of tropical grass with jointed stems, is found in many shapes and sizes.
2. The camel's body is adapted for the rigors of the desert.
3. The brain of a calculator, which is embedded in a layer of protective plastic, is almost indestructible.
4. In the spring the desert exploded with color.
5. The value of my garden extends far beyond what it produces.

Chapter 8
Writing a Composition or a Report

Page 147, Exercise A (The order of the ideas under each general heading may vary.)

    I. pedestrians often cause their own injuries
        they cross streets diagonally
        they cross streets in the middle of the block
        they walk with their backs to traffic on the highway
        they step into traffic from parked cars
        they step from behind parked cars
        they cross against lights
        they don't watch for traffic
   II. pedestrian lives can be saved
        provide adequate street lighting
        provide traffic lights for pedestrians
        give traffic tickets to pedestrians

Page 148, Exercise B (The order of the ideas under each general heading may vary.)

    I. description of career
        opportunities
        kinds of work involved
        places where such work is done
   II. qualifications needed
        specific attitudes
        physical and personal qualities
        education and other training
  III. rewards of this career
        service to society
        income
        personal satisfaction

Page 150, Exercise A

   1. MARKET GARDENING (chronological order)

      I. Deciding what to plant
     II. Selecting seed
   III. Preparing the soil
   IV. Planting

      V. Cultivating
     VI. Gathering the products
    VII. Preparing the products for market
   VIII. Selling the products

2. TENNIS: A GOOD GAME FOR STUDENTS (order of importance) (The order of the general headings and the order of the ideas under them may vary.)

  I. Pleasure
    A. Relaxation from study
    B. Interaction with others
    C. Joy of competition

  II. Health
    A. Increase in mental alertness
    B. Improvement in circulatory system

3. AUTOMOBILES SHOULD BE BANNED FROM CITIES (order of importance) (The order of the general headings and the order of the ideas under them may vary.)

   I. Public transportation is more efficient than the automobile.
    A. Automobiles are inefficient for moving large numbers of people.
    B. Many automobiles carry only one driver.
   II. The automobile is a nuisance and a health hazard.
    A. The automobile is the major source of air pollution.
    B. Accidents involving pedestrians and automobiles are common.
    C. Automobiles contribute to noise pollution.
  III. Dependence on automobiles hurts everyone.
    A. New freeways remove more land from residential, business, and recreational use.
    B. Money spent on new roads and road repairs could be put to better use elsewhere.

Page 161, Exercise A

1. repetition of the name V*ed* and the pronoun *I*
2. use of the word *same* to show relationship between ideas; repetition of the word *control*, the use of the words *discovered* and *discovery*
3. use of *mysterious catastrophe* as a kind of synonym for *too little rain*; use of time phrase *in the seventh year*
4. use of pronouns *she* and *her* to refer to Marget; repetition of word *class*
5. use of *the little creek* as synonym for *a thread of clear water*
6. repetition of pronoun *I*; use of *her* to refer to *Drusilla*
7. use of *later* to indicate time; use of *she* to refer to *Ollie*

Chapter 10
Letters, Applications, and Résumés

Page 208, Exercise A

1. Western Airlines Vacation Department
   P.O. Box 92931
   World Way Postal Center
   Los Angeles, California 90009

   Ladies and Gentlemen:
   (or Gentlemen:)
   (or Dear Sir or Madam:)

2. Personnel Manager
   General Telephone Co. of Florida
   610 Morgan Street
   Tampa, Florida 33602

   Dear Sir or Madam:
   (or Dear Sir:)
   (or Dear Madam:)

3. Quantas
   360 Post Street
   San Francisco, California 94108

   Ladies and Gentlemen:
   (or Gentlemen:)
   (or Dear Sir or Madam:)

4. Employment Office
   Yellowstone Company
   Yellowstone Park, Wyoming 82190

   Dear Sir or Madam:
   (or Ladies and Gentlemen:)
   (or Gentlemen:)

5. Admissions Office
   Colorado Women's College
   Montview Boulevard and Quebec
   Denver, Colorado 80220

   Dear Sir or Madam:
   (or Ladies and Gentlemen:)
   (or Gentlemen:)

Chapter 11
Using the Library and Reference Works

Page 234, Exercise A

1. 600   3. 700   5. 800   7. 600   9. 700
2. 300   4. 200   6. 900   8. 900   10. 300

Page 234, Exercise B

1. 200   3. 300   5. 100   7. 400   9. 500
2. 800   4. 900   6. 700   8. 900   10. 300

Page 238, Exercise A

4 *Don Quixote*
1 Badminton
1 *A Bell for Adano*
3 City Planning
1 *An American Dilemma*
2 Charlotte Brontë

5 *The Environmental Handbook*
1 Acting
1 Charles Beard
6 *A Friend of Caesar*

Page 239, Exercise C (Answers may vary somewhat.)

1. Bali—Social Life and Customs
2. Presidents—U.S.—Powers and Duties
3. Jewelry
4. Insurance, Automobile
5. Term Paper or Research Paper
6. Diet
7. Witchcraft
8. U.S.—History—Civil War—Ballads
9. Mars (Planet)
10. Submarines—History

Page 247, Exercise B

1. *Motown* is a shortened form of Motor Town, the nickname for Detroit.
2. the highest point of a mast; information about a newspaper or magazine (its name, notice of ownership, names of officers, address, and so on) printed at the head of the first column of the editorial page or elsewhere in monthly publications

3. strong, substantial, forceful, effective (Answers may vary.)
4. Southern United States
5. an informal or omitted leave-taking; expression evolved from the 18th century French custom of leaving a social gathering without taking leave of the host and hostess
6. (Answers will vary.)
7. an official appointed to investigate grievances against the government
8. a story used to teach or explain moral concept or idea (Examples will vary.)
9. musical instrument, shaped like a violin, with metal strings; played by striking it with two small hammers or by plucking it with a pick or quill
10. Radio Detecting and Ranging

Page 248, Exercise C (Answers taken from 1980 edition of *World Almanac.*)

1. Write Commissioner of Patents and Trademarks, Washington, D.C., 20231
2. 53 West Jackson Blvd., Chicago, Illinois 60604
3. all days, especially legal holidays, near polling places, in or near official buildings, and in or near schools in session; customary from sunrise to sunset and at night on special occasions
4. 8
5. lowered voting age to 18
6. first telephone call between New York and San Francisco by Alexander Graham Bell and Thomas A. Watson
7. Valentina V. Tereshkova
8. May 1986
9. 2:00 a.m. the following day
10. Washington

Page 248, Exercise D

1. Ap—April
   il—illustrated, illustration, illustrator
   +—continued on later pages of same issue
   por—portrait
   S—September
   Ag—August
   Ja—January
   supp—supplement
   tr—translated, translation, translator
   Jl—July

   abr—abridged
   jt auth—
       joint author

2. Motor T—*Motor Trend*
   Eng J—*English Journal*
   Sports Illus—*Sports Illustrated*
   Good H—*Good Housekeeping*
   Sat R—*Saturday Review*
   Sci Am—*Scientific American*
   Sr Schol—*Senior Scholastic*
   Phys Today—*Physics Today*
   U S News—*U.S. News & World Report*
   Bus-W—*Business Week*

Page 249, Exercise E (Sources may vary.)

1. (Answers will vary.)
2. played a leading role in the Continental Congress; wrote the Declaration of Independence; served as lawmaker in Virginia during the war years (*World Book Encyclopedia*)
3. "Fire and Ice" by Robert Frost (*Granger's Index to Poetry*)
4. (Photographs will vary.)
5. When drinking tea in a garden, Newton saw an apple fall, and at that moment he realized that the same force that pulled the apple to earth also keeps the rest of the world "pulled together" (*World Book Encyclopedia*)
6. expression meaning "the real thing"; taken from the name of the nineteenth century inventor who perfected a lubricating device for machinery that eliminated costly shut-downs; expression derived from the insistence of machinery buyers that only McCoy lubricators be installed on new equipment (*World Book Encyclopedia*)
7. 50 sites (*World Book Encyclopedia*)
8. a group of European and American dramatists of the 1950's and 1960's who had in common a belief in the essential absurdity of life (*Reader's Encyclopedia of World Drama*)
9. *Plot Guide to 100 British and American Novels* (Answers may vary.)
10. Walt Whitman (*American Anthology* 1787–1900), born in West Hills, Long Island, New York in 1819 (*Dictionary of American Biography*)

Handbook

Section 1
The Classification of Words

Page 263, Exercise A

1. announcer, plane, Minneapolis, minutes
2. Dr. Cooper, college, mother
3. John, ribbon, typewriter, ribbon
4. scream, tires, thud, sound, glass
5. Carl, brother, continent, car
6. boys, desert, night
7. Helen, president, class, brother, secretary
8. Al, paper, Babe Didrikson, life, sports
9. Half, people, world
10. Georgia O'Keefe, paintings, desert

Page 263, Exercise B

1. German, English
2. Lake Erie, Mount Everest
3. Joshua National Monument, Cape Cod
4. Fairfield Township, Saint Paul
5. Labor Day, Good Friday
6. Senator Nancy Kassebaum, Mayor Tom Bradley
7. Justice Thurgood Marshall, Judge Shirley M. Hufstedler
8. Uncle Harry, Rittenhouse Square, Boston Common
9. Saint Patrick's Cathedral
10. Dartmouth College, Jefferson High School

Page 266, Exercise

1. they (boys); his (doctor)
2. your (Bob); you (Bob), him (father)
3. They (Helen and Karen); it (test)
4. its (crowd)
5. her (Ali); them (ideas)
6. its (spacecraft)
7. their (boys); their (boys)
8. him (Jim); theirs (neighbors)

9. she (Betty); it (permit), her (Betty)
10. they (police); it (car)

Page 267, Exercise

1. herself or himself (doctor)
2. themselves (students)
3. herself (Eve)
4. himself (Harry)
5. yourselves (girls)
6. himself (Jack)
7. yourself (Jane)
8. themselves (boys)
9. ourselves (we)
10. himself or herself (president)

Page 269, Exercise A

1. Nobody—indefinite
2. her—personal
3. Some—indefinite
4. All—indefinite
5. Who—interrogative; their—personal
6. Someone—indefinite; her—personal
7. What—interrogative; you—personal
8. This—demonstrative
9. this—demonstrative; you—personal
10. you—personal; anything—indefinite

Page 270, Exercise B

1. Which—interrogative; these—demonstrative, yours—personal
2. Whom—interrogative
3. Many—indefinite; few—indefinite; it—personal
4. This—demonstrative; someone—indefinite
5. Anyone—indefinite
6. This—demonstrative
7. Everything—indefinite; I—personal
8. Neither—indefinite; anything—indefinite
9. That—demonstrative; anyone—indefinite
10. Several—indefinite; our—personal

Page 273, Exercise A

1. had seen
2. will be banned
3. was blinded
4. have had
5. will be
6. has been enforced
7. Do have
8. had run
9. had been painted
10. were nearing
11. was lifting
12. has returned
13. can be seen
14. Have been trying
15. was being exhausted

Page 273, Exercise B

1. sat—action
2. smelled—action
3. remained—linking
4. sounded—linking
5. sounded—action
6. lay—action
7. felt—action
8. seemed—linking
9. felt—linking
10. left—action
11. looked—action
12. appeared—action
13. looks—linking
14. appears—linking
15. seemed—linking

Page 276, Exercise A

1. has been doing—progressive
2. does seem—emphatic
3. are exploring—progressive
4. have been hoping—progressive
5. does save—emphatic
6. will be filing—progressive
7. do know—emphatic
8. have been working—progressive
9. Has been doing—progressive
10. did approve—emphatic

Page 276, Exercise B

1. arrived—intransitive
2. stepped—intransitive
3. has—transitive
4. walked—intransitive
5. tells—transitive
6. played—intransitive
7. struck—transitive
8. enjoys—transitive
9. does appear—intransitive
10. have—transitive

Page 277, Exercise C

1. had been turned—passive
2. have been invited—passive
3. has picked—active
4. was hit—passive

5. do understand—active
6. were played—passive
7. will be constructed—passive
8. told—active
9. have been discovered—passive
10. has bought—active

Page 277, Exercise D

1. The class president will introduce the speaker.
2. Our record has been equaled only by Woodbridge.
3. The gym was decorated by our class.
4. The school doctor gave the influenza shots.
5. The rain ruined the game.
6. A flat tire delayed the team bus.
7. Frost destroyed the citrus fruit.
8. The mayor will dedicate the new bridge.
9. The rock concert was interrupted by a flaming explosion.
10. My sister was elected president by her class.

Page 282, Exercise A

1. do know—present emphatic
2. handled—past
3. seems—present
4. stood—past
5 had vanished—past perfect
6. Will have—future
7. are finding—present progressive
8. will have grown—future perfect
9. had been behaving—past perfect
10. have been—present perfect

Page 282, Exercise B

1. had lived—past perfect
2. serves—present
3. will open—future
4. has won—present perfect
5. makes—present
6. won—past
7. has been organizing—present perfect progressive
8. will have passed—future perfect
9. was playing—past progressive
10. returned—past, had played—past perfect

Page 285, Exercise A

1. old, empty (house); several (years)
2. second (team); last (quarter)
3. new, patient, helpful (teacher)
4. poor (elephant); bad (toothache)

5. enormous (jet); small (airport)
6. magnetic (field); entire (earth)
7. new, atomic, spacious, comfortable (submarines)
8. this (lake); salty (water)
9. Many, young (Americans); scientific (discoveries)
10. two, angry (people); other (car)

Page 285, Exercise B

1. This, little (book); some, big (ideas)
2. cold (wind); deep (snow); huge (drifts)
3. young (jockey); many (races)
4. sixteen, different (coins)
5. This, new (tent); several (people)
6. Most, European (students); English (language)
7. overdue (books)
8. dry, gritty (hamburger)
9. Some, small, economy, small, economical (cars)
10. famous (Janet Guthrie); first, woman (racer)

Page 287, Exercise A

1. best—superlative
2. bigger—comparative
3. mightier—comparative
4. fastest—superlative
5. most unhappy—superlative
6. more plentiful—comparative
7. harder—comparative
8. larger—comparative
9. worst—superlative
10. largest—superlative

Page 287, Exercise B

1. larger—comparative
2. worse—comparative
3. higher—comparative
4. funnier—comparative
5. fastest—superlative
6. last—superlative
7. most intriguing—superlative
8. most comfortable—superlative
9. more appealing—comparative
10. most hilarious—superlative

Page 290, Exercise A

1. almost (always); always (arrives); late (arrives)
2. hard (worked); successfully (worked)
3. usually (does start); easily (does start)
4. rather (crowded); recently (have become)

5. soon (was filled);
   completely (was filled)
6. nearly (every)
7. quietly (gave);
8. sometimes (is);
   rather (difficult)
9. Lately (have been);
   extremely (hot)
10. There (goes);
    now (goes)

Page 290, Exercise B

1. carefully (approached)
2. yesterday (Did send)
3. Soon (had finished)
4. now (was);
   nearly (exhausted)
5. eagerly (raised)
6. often had (explored);
   before (had explored)
7. recently (have discovered)
8. almost (completely);
   completely (flooded)
9. suddenly (became)
10. quietly (come);
    outside (leave)

Page 292, Exercise A

1. at (border); for (arms)
2. During (centuries)
3. to (stage); at (audience)
4. To (whom)
5. After (game); for (exists)
6. According to (paper); on (Friday)
7. of (Quebec); instead of (English)
8. Beyond (limits); against
   (fireworks)
9. At (half time); onto (field)
10. For (years); in (disrepair)

Page 292, Exercise B

1. On (weekends); for (neighbors)
2. at (Washington Zoo); on (diets)
3. around (kitchen); for (dinner)
4. over (piles); of (garbage)
5. but (Marietta)
6. above (trees)
7. after (talk); with (coach)
8. but (one); of (trees); during
   (winter)
9. Instead of (bus); to (school)
10. Aside from (cost); to (proposal)

Page 295, Exercise A

1. Neither/nor (correlative)
2. Both/and (correlative)
3. and (coordinating)
4. either/or (correlative)
5. but (coordinating)
6. Although (subordinating)
7. when (subordinating)
8. nonetheless (conjunctive adverb)

9. however (conjunctive adverb)
10. When (subordinating)
11. whenever (subordinating)
12. otherwise (conjunctive adverb)

13. provided (subordinating)
14. so that (subordinating)
15. but (coordinating)

Page 295, Exercise B

1. but (joins adjectives)
2. Neither/nor (joins nouns)
3. but (joins clauses)
4. and (joins nouns)
5. but (joins adjectives)

6. and (joins prepositional phrases)
7. and (joins noun phrases)
8. either/or (joins nouns)
9. not only/but also (joins adjectives)
10. both /and (joins nouns)

Page 299, Exercise A

1. preposition
2. conjunction
3. preposition
4. conjunction
5. preposition

6. conjunction
7. pronoun
8. adjective
9. adjective
10. pronoun

11. adjective, adverb
12. preposition
13. adverb
14. preposition
15. adverb

Page 299, Exercise B

1. noun
2. pronoun
3. adverb
4. adjective
5. adverb

6. adjective
7. noun
8. adjective
9. adverb
10. adjective, pronoun

11. noun
12. adjective
13. verb
14. noun
15. verb

Page 302, Exercise A

1. to help
2. to survey the bottom of the oceans
3. to accept the challenge
4. to work on the problem slowly and carefully
5. to pick up sounds far out in space
6. to be invited to the dinner
7. to be told the truth

8. to have had two parts
9. to have been invited
10. to have been broken
11. To gain admission to the Air Force Academy
12. to be given fuller directions
13. to end the party at midnight
14. to hear the election returns
15. to be a writer

Page 303, Exercise B

1. to leave now
2. to telephone home
3. to be late
4. to be broken
5. to have been cut deliberately
6. to wash its food
7. to be sure of the facts
8. to help you with your tennis
9. To get a better view
10. to come to our house for supper

Page 304, Exercise A

1. Walking
2. Making a speech
3. standing in line
4. Quick thinking
5. painting the house herself
6. raking leaves
7. Making new friends
8. Spending more than you earn
9. Horseback riding
10. cooking Chinese food in a wok
11. mowing lawns
12. studying on the bus
13. backing down the hill
14. winning her race
15. leaving the city

Page 305, Exercise B

1. managing money
2. Studying, boxing
3. Disco dancing
4. making decisions
5. Pleasing the crowds
6. talking too loud
7. waiting patiently for an hour
8. barking
9. The constant dripping of water
10. skin diving

Page 306, Exercise A

1. Running at great speed (Pat)
2. straining every muscle (cyclist)
3. trying for a double (runner)
4. Working fast (Julia)
5. Smelling smoke (Coretta)
6. Surrounded by enemy ships (Drake)
7. pleased with Grasso's victory (crowd)
8. loaded with gold nuggets (prospectors)
9. waiting for a verdict (defendant)
10. Having been defeated twice (Purdue)
11. topped with marshmallows (sundae)
12. Walking carefully on the rocks (hikers)
13. knocking over a stack of cans (toddler)

14. ripping up her math homework (terrier)
15. Trained for emergencies (paramedics)

Page 307, Exercise B

1. Concentrating on his form (Roger)
2. shown on television (violence)
3. Outdistancing her guard (Jane), scoring easily (Jane)
4. carrying their injured friend (miners), injured (friend)
5. careening wildly (boat)
6. stricken with grief (cobbler)
7. Struck by a sudden idea (Sally)
8. Having twice won the prize (Hal)
9. determined to win (team)
10. worn (sign), battered by wind and rain (sign)

Page 307, Exercise C

1. Taking—gerund
2. to take—infinitive
3. running—gerund
4. unexpected—participle
5. to dance—infinitive
6. to improve—infinitive
7. Playing—gerund
8. Disappointed—participle
9. Having—gerund
10. Having passed—participle
11. clowning—gerund
12. to study—infinitive
13. Ignoring—participle
14. to succeed—infinitive
15. turning—participle

Page 308, Review: The Classification of Words

1. Several—pronoun; on—preposition
2. soon—adverb; plant—noun; three—adjective
3. Although—conjunction; seemed—verb; nervous—adjective
4. Wow—interjection; That—pronoun
5. keeper—noun; sounded—verb
6. are finding—verb; uses—noun; laser—adjective
7. guided—verb; along —preposition
8. his—adjective; going—gerund
9. ate—verb; some—pronoun
10. Who—pronoun; Antarctica—noun
11. Ashley—noun; palms—noun
12. or—conjunction; nearly—adverb
13. Frequently—adverb; uses—verb; to exercise—infinitive
14. while—conjunction; for—preposition
15. Aha—interjection; one—pronoun

Section 2
The Parts of a Sentence

Page 310, Exercise A

The following groups of words are sentences: 2, 7, 9, 13, and 14.

Page 310, Exercise B

The following groups of words are sentences: 1, 4, 8, 11, 14, and 15.

Page 312, Exercise A

1. interrogative
2. declarative
3. imperative
4. interrogative
5. imperative
6. exclamatory
7. interrogative
8. declarative
9. declarative
10. exclamatory

Page 312, Exercise B

1. interrogative
2. imperative
3. declarative
4. exclamatory
5. interrogative
6. declarative
7. imperative
8. imperative
9. declarative
10. imperative

Page 314, Exercise A

1. verb—won; subject—Robert Frost
2. verb—have won; subject—Yankees
3. verb—flowed; subjects—Streams, rivers
4. verbs—orbits, circles; subject—rocket
5. verb—are recording; subjects—Carly Simon, James Taylor
6. verbs—swayed, danced; subject—trees
7. verb—are displayed; subjects—silks, cottons
8. verbs—rose, stretched, shook; subject—dog
9. verb—helped; subject—members
10. verb—filled; subjects—Oranges, grapes, boxes

Page 315, Exercise B

1. verb—make; subjects—Soup, fruit, bread
2. verb—are; subject—possessions
3. verb—have organized; subject—schools
4. verb—Are; subjects—Natalia Makarova, Cynthia Gregory
5. verb—had come; subjects—she, friend
6. verbs—took, flew; subject—pigeons
7. verbs—changed, fidgeted, left; subject—He
8. verb—depressed; subjects—chill, dampness
9. verb—will sing; subjects—soprano, alto
10. verb—had turned; subjects—punishment, flogging

Page 317, Exercise A

1. verb—came; subject—"bravos"
2. verb—did lose; subject—you
3. verb—Could have seen; subject—you
4. verb—are; subject—keys
5. verb—rose; subject—moon
6. verb—crept; subject—cat
7. verb—was; subject—house
8. verb—Should have telephoned; subject—I
9. verb—might have been; subject—accident
10. verb—leaped; subject—kangaroo

Page 317, Exercise B

1. verb—came; subject—hoot
2. verb—lay; subject—scarf
3. verb—came; subject—trucks
4. verb—Did see; subject—you
5. verb—Have heard; subject—you
6. verb—came; subject—sound
7. verb—can enjoy; subject—you
8. verb—will be; subject—drill
9. verb—was; subject—prize
10. verb—will hear; subject—sister

Page 320, Exercise A

	DIRECT OBJECT	INDIRECT OBJECT
1.	card	Doreen
2.	advice	council
3.	letter	mayor
4.	job	Ward

DIRECT OBJECT	INDIRECT OBJECT
5. month	you
6. excuse	teacher
7. lift	boys
8. eraser	Suzanne
9. program	me
10. job	Sonia

Page 320, Exercise B

DIRECT OBJECT	INDIRECT OBJECT
1. floods	Texas
2. ticket	sister
3. scholarships	students
4. recommendations	Congress
5. paintings	visitors
6. wishes	you
7. supplies	party
8. slides	us
9. citation	ship
10. farewell	islanders

Page 322, Exercise A

1. chance
2. modern
3. happy
4. full
5. president
6. opportunity
7. sight
8. exciting
9. friend
10. player

Page 322, Exercise B

	SUBJECT	VERB	DIRECT OBJECT	INDIRECT OBJECT	PREDICATE WORD
1.	commander	gave	warning	troops	
2.	We	have	settlement		
3.	Jane Oliver	gave	autograph	us	
4.	cars	piled			
5.	Jim	Has read	directions		
6.	jets	are			sensitive
7.	towns	appear			
8.	men	rowed	boat		
9.	plane	was chased			

SUBJECT	VERB	DIRECT OBJECT	INDIRECT OBJECT	PREDICATE WORD
10. Dr. Johnson	wrote	excuse		
11. rebels	appear			confident
12. shop	has made	table	us	
13. Deerfield	scored	touchdowns		
14. sources	will change	lives		
15. leaders	were			scientists

Page 324, Exercise

1. washed, waxed (verb)
2. struck the runway, bounced high in the air (predicate)
3. tired, unhappy (predicate word)
4. led the orchestra, played the piano (predicate)
5. record, letters (direct object)
6. bright, colorful (predicate word)
7. patrols, parties (subject)
8. Nile, Amazon, Mississippi (predicate word)
9. passengers, crew (subject)
10. baited his hook, tossed out his line (predicate)
11. blue, gold (predicate word)
12. Fame, fortune (subject)
13. arrived, looked (verb)
14. loyalty, sympathy, patience (direct object)
15. Tugs, fireboats, liners (subject)

Page 328, Exercise A

1. In the late afternoon (had)
2. of applause (burst)
3. on the Yukon River (had been lost); for three days (had been lost)
4. in a box (had been hidden); of rubbish (box)
5. at the museum (can work); after school (can work)
6. of the leading lady (illness); in our plans (change)
7. For twenty years (captured); in the iron mask (man)
8. Before a holiday (pervades); of excitement (feeling)
9. of smoke (cloud); on the horizon (appeared)
10. For two hours (clung); to the rock (clung); with her fingertips (clung)

Page 328, Exercise B

1. in the morning (Early); at the lake (arrived)
2. in the middle (was); of the night (middle)

3. for a distance (visible); of ten miles (distance)
4. Below the North Pole (has); of nearly three miles (depth)
5. At the South Pole (is); of ice (mass)
6. During the storm (hurled); onto the shore (hurled)
7. with her mother (went); in the afternoon (went)
8. of angry people (crowd); outside the store (gathered)
9. Before the railroads (traveled); along the rivers (traveled)
10. For years (towed); over the mountains (towed)

Page 330, Exercise A

1. to leave town
2. to win this election
3. to read *Sounder* for her report
4. to get letters from the voters
5. to get a job next summer
6. to rent their house for the summer
7. to paint the fence
8. to be hard working
9. to watch Babe Ruth
10. To pay his debts, to sell his library

Page 330, Exercise B

1. to write for a newspaper
2. To study for the test
3. to halt inflation
4. to see the King Tut exhibit
5. To open the garage door
6. to live in the White House
7. To keep plants healthy
8. to be more frightening than *Jaws*
9. To clean the attic
10. to sing along

Page 332, Exercise A

1. Arriving in Philadelphia (Franklin)
2. Having finished her required work (Cara)
3. disguised in strange clothing (Lincoln)
4. Alarmed by the condition of the troops (general)
5. Appearing before the committee (accountant)

6. wilting under the hot sun (pros)
7. carrying a mysterious package (girls)
8. convinced of his defeat (Woodrow Wilson)
9. Having studied the chapter thoroughly (I)
10. determined to finish the game (Lynn)

Page 332, Exercise B

1. Panting heavily (Kris)
2. driving the tractors (people)
3. riding the ten-speed bicycle (woman)
4. having finished their work (nurses)
5. waiting for the show to begin (audience)
6. Best known for her novels (Willa Cather)
7. intended for a general audience (Movies)
8. scoring the most points (player)
9. posted on the bulletin board (notice)
10. Seared by the drought (farms)

Page 334, Exercise A

1. Cooking
2. painting in their spare hours
3. shopping carefully
4. Courteous driving
5. studying
6. hearing your speech
7. Getting there
8. losing the game
9. going to bed
10. Sleeping late on Saturdays
11. closing the camp
12. reading comic books
13. playing chess
14. Climbing the fence
15. Watching the clock

Page 335, Exercise B

1. sitting—participle
2. wounded—participle
3. to fly—infinitive; taking—gerund
4. Lost—participle; lying—participle
5. hoping—participle, to talk—infinitive
6. to mine—infinitive
7. to see—infinitive
8. landing—gerund; to wait—infinitive
9. finding—gerund; to survive—infinitive
10. to pay—infinitive; working—gerund

Page 342, Exercise A

1. Pattern Two	5. Pattern Four	8. Pattern Two
2. Pattern One	6. Pattern Five	9. Pattern Four
3. Pattern Three	7. Pattern Three	10. Pattern One
4. Pattern Five		

Page 342, Exercise B

1. Pattern Five	5. Pattern Five	8. Pattern Four
2. Pattern One	6. Pattern Three	9. Pattern Two
3. Pattern One	7. Pattern Three	10. Pattern Two
4. Pattern Four		

Page 342, Exercise C (Sentences will vary.)

Page 343, Review: The Parts of a Sentence

	SUBJECT	VERB	DIRECT OBJECT	INDIRECT OBJECT	PREDICATE WORD	PREPOSITIONAL PHRASE
1.	class	wrote, produced	musical			
2.	aunt	sent	piñata, sombrero	me		in Mexico
3.	snowfall	stopped	trains, buses			in the city
4.	defendant	admitted	guilt			During the trial
5.	bob-sledding	is			event	in the Olympics
6.	magician	showed	tricks	Willy		
7.	class	wore	togas			for a Roman banquet
8.	babysitter	gave	crackers, cheese	children		
9.	ride	was			short	
10.	Pigs, cattle	were loaded				onto railroad cars
11.	cave	seems			eerie, hazardous	
12.	gust	scattered	homework			of wind, around the parking lot

	SUBJECT	VERB	DIRECT OBJECT	INDIRECT OBJECT	PREDICATE WORD	PREPOSITIONAL PHRASE
13.	airplanes	performed	stunts			for the crowd
14.	coach	spotted	Kendra			during her backflip
15.	R. L. Jeffries	is			supervisor	at the glassworks
16.	Billie Holiday	was			singer	
17.	Cindy	asked	questions	veterinarian		about proper pet care
18.	Dad	taught	dive	us		
19.	Cassie	seems			confused	about the algebra assignment
20.	class	did elect	Whom			for president

Section 3

Sentence and Clause

Page 345, Exercise A

1. manager, assistant—compound subject
2. left the house early, walked to school—compound predicate
3. will hire an orchestra, arrange for decorations—compound predicate
4. designed, painted—compound verb
5. Strawberries, asparagus—compound subject
6. spark, sputter—compound verb
7. read several books about Marie Curie, wrote a report about the famous chemist—compound predicate
8. filled the gas tank, checked the oil—compound predicate
9. guitarist, player—compound subject
10. Hamilton, Washington—compound subject

Page 346, Exercise B

1. examined the old paintings, declared them priceless—compound predicate
2. rabbit, dog—compound subject
3. decorated their bikes, wore costumes—compound predicate
4. you, Evan—compound subject
5. add, subtract, multiply, divide—compound verb

6. removes the ends, flattens the metal—compound predicate
7. looked up, gave an order to one of the aides—compound predicate
8. Bells, sirens, whistles—compound subject
9. skidded, whined—compound verb
10. mounted his horse, rode through the snow alone to his beloved home at Monticello—compound predicate

Page 349, Exercise A

1. compound
2. simple; compound predicate—can start French this year, wait until next year
3. simple; compound predicate—left the launching pad, vanished into the upper sky
4. compound
5. compound
6. simple; compound predicate—can take a train tonight, fly to Detroit in the morning
7. simple; compound predicate—ate all of his food, complained about every bite
8. compound
9. simple; compound predicate—visited the Museum of Modern Art, spent hours studying the new paintings
10. compound

Page 349, Exercise B

1. simple; compound predicate—turns on its axis every twenty-eight days, therefore always presents the same face to the earth
2. compound
3. compound
4. compound
5. simple; compound predicate—reduce back-breaking labor, increase production
6. compound
7. simple; compound predicate—attend college, do not stay to graduate
8. simple; compound predicate—dropped its program after the death of a football player, did not start it again until last year
9. compound
10. simple; compound predicate—sat by the telephone all evening, drove everyone else away.

Page 351, Exercise

1. phrase   3. phrase   5. phrase
2. clause   4. phrase   6. clause

7. clause	10. clause	13. phrase
8. phrase	11. phrase	14. clause
9. phrase	12. clause	15. phrase

Page 352, Exercise A

1. where the accident occurred
2. that you wanted
3. who sent the flowers
4. before you go to bed
5. Unless the rain stops
6. where the Millers live
7. after the Erie Canal opened
8. who bought our house
9. if the power fails
10. When there is a heavy snowfall in the city.

Page 353, Exercise B

1. complex	5. compound	8. complex
2. complex	6. simple	9. simple
3. simple	7. simple	10. complex
4. compound		

Page 356, Exercise A

1. when you can see meteors (month)
2. you bought yesterday (record)
3. who won the gold medal (skater)
4. where the first state capitol stood (spot)
5. to whom we wrote (person)
6. that no one had ever seen (buildings)
7. that come from outer space (objects)
8. you are using (energy)
9. who are honest and fearless (leaders)
10. that ever happened to you (thing)

Page 356, Exercise B

1. when you should avoid the roads (time)
2. that sells running shoes (store)
3. that does not produce heat (light)

4. we are planning (trip)
5. which has only 925 students (school)
6. of which I was speaking (chapter)
7. you need (everything)
8. that you might enjoy (book) or (poems)
9. that we ordered in September (books)
10. to whom you spoke (lady)

Page 359, Exercise A

1. When the girls returned to Paris (sold)
2. As soon as the snow starts falling (go)
3. Whenever there is an accident (gathers)
4. While she was studying for the test (ate)
5. while Martin cooked the hamburgers (set)
6. as Diane Pulcinski went to bat (was hushed)
7. As soon as the ride started (were shrieking)
8. where the soil is sandy (grow)
9. until the spring thaws come (are isolated)
10. Unless more funds are raised (will have)

Page 359, Exercise B

1. Since this was his first meeting (said)
2. if you don't like it (may return)
3. When the judge entered (stood)
4. While the car was being repaired (walked)
5. Because the snowstorm halted all buses (was canceled)
6. when you have time (Could help)
7. when the Panama Canal treaty was signed (rejoiced)
8. because his Aunt Sally wants to "civilize" him (leaves)
9. until he was nineteen (has flown)
10. as we approached the house (was)

Page 362, Exercise A

1. where she had been—object of verb *would tell*
2. What the reporter really wanted—subject of *was*
3. what he had said—object of preposition *for*
4. that Marion could get up tomorrow—object of verb *said*
5. who invented the microscope—object of verb *Do know*

6. what might happen—object of preposition *of*
7. who wrote the threatening letters—object of verb *know*
8. Who will win the game—subject of *is*
9. that the test would be difficult—object of verb *knew*
10. the day would never end—object of the verb *thought*
11. What happened to the missing artist—subject of verb *was never discovered*
12. whatever you can do—object of preposition *for*
13. what you want—object of verb *can get*
14. Jim had such powers of concentration—object of verb *did know*
15. what you expected—predicate noun

Page 362, Exercise B

1. adjective	6. adverb	11. noun
2. noun	7. adjective	12. adjective
3. adverb	8. adverb	13. adverb
4. noun	9. noun	14. adjective
5. adjective	10. adverb	15. noun

Page 364, Review: Sentence and Clause

1. complex; how she weaves cloth on a loom—noun clause
2. complex; as it pulled away—adverb clause
3. simple
4. compound
5. simple
6. complex; that contained two dozen eggs—adjective clause
7. complex; if there is rain—adverb clause
8. compound
9. complex; while the band members marched—adverb clause
10. compound
11. complex; when Steve Martin appeared on stage—adverb clause
12. complex; What annoys Mr. Berman most—noun clause
13. simple
14. complex; Unless it is threatened—adverb clause
15. compound
16. complex; While everyone slept—adverb clause
17. compound
18. compound
19. simple
20. complex; that was ever printed—adjective clause

Section 4

Complete Sentences

1. Then came Tom, wearing a wide-brimmed hat and a false mustache.
2. The network replaced that show with a program just like several others.
3. After reaching the top of the last hill, we stopped to rest.
4. Most of the great books are available in inexpensive paperbacks.
5. Mr. Walters is one of the oldest residents in the city.
6. The huge trucks are rolling along the nation's highways all night.
7. Finally, in a corner of the garage, the missing wrenches were found.
8. There was nothing in the newspapers about the robbery.
9. There is a reward for anyone who finds the valuable bracelet.
10. After working hard all day, we welcomed a little relaxation.

Page 367, Exercise B (Sentence completions will vary.)

1. fragment—There are ghost towns all across the country.
2. Fragment—Pithole, Pennsylvania, is one of the most famous ghost towns.
3. Complete sentence.
4. Fragment—For a time, 20,400 people lived in the town.
5. Complete sentence.
6. Fragment—Elsewhere ghost towns are found in timber country.
7. Fragment—Modern ghost towns are in the iron-mining regions of Minnesota.
8. Fragment—The most famous of all the ghost towns are in the mining sections of the West.
9. Fragment—There are houses full of furniture and offices with papers in the desks.
10. Complete sentence.

Page 368, Exercise A (Sentence completions will vary.)

1. fragment—Except me. Everyone, except me, liked the banana cream pie.
2. fragment—Another bad accident on the highway. Once again the sirens wailed because there was another bad accident on the highway.

3. fragment—For many years. Grace has been interested in music for many years.

4. fragment—Just before midnight. We finally arrived just before midnight.

5. fragment—Before signing the treaty. Before signing the treaty, the President said a few words.

6. fragment—As soon as possible. Please send your order as soon as possible.

7. fragment—Hoping to improve her skills. Hoping to improve her skills, Linda joined the debate team.

8. fragment—Almost twenty-two hours each week. The average American teen-ager watches TV almost twenty-two hours each week.

9. fragment—From 9:00 to 10:30 A.M. The instructor taught yoga three days a week from 9:00 to 10:30 A.M.

10. fragments—Quarterback Ken Stabler, a leader in pass completions.—Plays for the Oakland Raiders. Quarterback Ken Stabler, a leader in pass completions, plays for the Oakland Raiders.

Page 369, Exercise B (Sentence completions will vary.)

1. fragment—Before the deadline? Did you finish your project before the deadline?

2. fragment—And his tape recorder. Larry sold his bike and his tape recorder.

3. fragment—Then the barn. The haystack and then the barn caught fire.

4. fragment—Including the Tidal Wave at Great America. An article rated the top ten roller coasters, including the Tidal Wave at Great America.

5. fragment—To work during the Eagles concert. Sixteen ushers were hired to work during the Eagles concert.

6. fragment—A natural talent. Alice played the piano so effortlessly that she seemed to have a natural talent.

7. fragment—A thrilling experience. Skiing on snow-covered mountains. Skiing on snow-covered mountains is a thrilling experience.

8. fragments—The plane, ready for take-off. Taxied down the runway. The plane, ready for take-off, taxied down the runway.

9. fragment—Scattering eggs all over. The truck had slid into the ditch, scattering eggs all over.

10. fragments—Katherine Graham, publisher of the *Washington Post*. A widely read newspaper. Katherine Graham is publisher of the *Washington Post*, a widely read newspaper.

Page 371, Exercise A (Sentence completions will vary.)

1. Margo arranged with the band leader for the musicians to play an extra hour.
2. The leader of the expedition is a scientist of wide experience.
3. Scientists are studying the ocean as a source of food and minerals.
4. The program, which we had seen before, gives a fascinating explanation of sound waves.
5. The bases were loaded, and Steve Garvey was at bat.
6. Jane is delighted with the chance to visit Hawaii.
7. The reporter asked Rep. Crane about running for President.
8. Pete and his friends are busy making plans for the hike.
9. Sally's great ambition is to become a surgeon.
10. Was *The Thorn Birds* made into a movie starring Robert Redford?

Page 371, Exercise B

1. The newspaper story contains an unfair statement of what had happened.
2. We waited in line to buy tickets for the Barry Manilow concert.
3. The two books, one a true story and the other a fictional account of Frémont's expedition, are both worth reading.
4. The *Mary Deare* was found drifting with no crew aboard.
5. There is an increasing need for food for the world's population.
6. Expecting no one to believe him, the boy told his story.
7. The class adviser arranged for a bus to take the group to the contest.
8. The Rose Bowl, The Gator Bowl, the Sun Bowl, the Orange Bowl, and the Cotton Bowl are only a few of football's "bowls."
9. The unhappy motorist was searching her pockets for her license.
10. The book gives an account of how the Spanish Armada was defeated.

Page 372, Exercise A (Sentence completions will vary.)

1. Beth is the only one who knew the answers.
2. The trapper stayed in the mountains until the first snow fell.
3. Since nobody else wanted it, she took the old painting.
4. Although the book is unusually long, it is worth reading.
5. There will be a big celebration in Pittsburgh when the Pirates win the pennant.
6. Because she likes outdoor life, Linda is studying forestry.
7. We were preparing a report on the rock collection that we had started the year before.
8. Ruth decided to buy the red coat even though her mother disliked it.

9. We will be glad to see you whenever you can come.
10. In the camp, the explorers checked their pitons, which are spikes used for climbing steep rock faces.

Page 373, Exercise B (Sentence completions will vary.)

1. At the age of thirty-three, Thomas Jefferson wrote the Declaration of Independence.
2. As she walks along, a mother rhinoceros always keeps her baby ahead of her.
3. India has over two hundred languages and many religions.
4. My library at home contains many paperbacks as well as books with beautiful, gold-tooled leather covers.
5. Ernest Hemingway wrote "The Killers," one of the most famous short stories of our time.
6. In a full orchestra, there are four families of instruments: stringed instruments, woodwinds, brasses, and percussion instruments.
7. She is one of those overly cautious people who are always raising objections.
8. Northern Canada is a vast Arctic waste with a few people, many caribou, and numerous fur-bearing animals.
9. The needle of a compass always points north because it is attracted by a center of magnetic force near the North Pole.
10. Edison's first electric light bulb burned for forty hours. Today the average life of a 100-watt bulb is over 750 hours.

Page 375, Exercise A (Following are the three acceptable revivisions of each run-on.)

1. We flew to Idaho Falls. Then we took a bus to the lake.
   We flew to Idaho Falls; then we took a bus to the lake.
   We flew to Idaho Falls, and then we took a bus to the lake.
2. Andy tries to practice the flute every day. However, he doesn't always have time.
   Andy tries to practice the flute every day; however, he doesn't always have time.
   Andy tries to practice the flute every day, but he doesn't always have time.
3. Ms. Albrecht has a new car. It is a Plymouth Horizon.
   Ms. Albrecht has a new car; it is a Plymouth Horizon.
   Ms. Albrecht has a new car, and it is a Plymouth Horizon.
4. Cooking a turkey takes several hours. Therefore, it has to be started early.

Cooking a turkey takes several hours; therefore, it has to be started early.

Cooking a turkey takes several hours, and it has to be started early.

5. Howard University is small. Nevertheless, it has an excellent faculty.

Howard University is small; nevertheless, it has an excellent faculty.

Howard University is small, but it has an excellent faculty.

6. The station was crowded. We nearly missed our train.

The station was crowded; we nearly missed our train.

The station was crowded, and we nearly missed our train.

7. It isn't a new dress. I wore it to the Christmas party.

It isn't a new dress; I wore it to the Christmas party.

It isn't a new dress, for I wore it to the Christmas party.

8. Pat hasn't called. He must be lost.

Pat hasn't called; he must be lost.

Pat hasn't called, and he must be lost.

9. We organized a benefit dance. However, the band never showed up.

We organized a benefit dance; however, the band never showed up.

We organized a benefit dance, but the band never showed up.

10. Mom painted the chairs. They look very nice.

Mom painted the chairs; they look very nice.

Mom painted the chairs, and they look very nice.

11. Mark is color-blind. Therefore, his wife always buys his ties.

Mark is color-blind; therefore, his wife always buys his ties.

Mark is color-blind, and his wife always buys his ties.

12. You take the general course first. Then you can specialize.

You take the general course first; then you can specialize.

You take the general course first, and then you can specialize.

13. The fog was very heavy. No planes left the airport.

The fog was very heavy; no plane left the airport.

The fog was very heavy, and no planes left the airport.

14. Larry started to cross the street. Then the light changed.

Larry started to cross the street; then the light changed.

Larry started to cross the street, and then the light changed.

15. Jim hesitated too long. Consequently, he missed his chance.

Jim hesitated too long; consequently, he missed his chance.

Jim hesitated too long, and, consequently, he missed his chance.

Page 375, Exercise B (These sentences are sample completions. Sentences will vary.)

1. The deer started to cross the road; then it stopped when it heard a noise.

2. The author of the article is Woody Allen; he is always amusing.

3. We were not expecting you today; however, we are happy you came.

4. The road was strewn with heavy branches; it was impassable.
5. The class had had plenty of time to study; nonetheless, they failed the exam.
6. Jan and Sylvia were late to class, but they had a pass.
7. The driver had simply been going too fast; moreoever, he had been drinking.
8. The town's population has been declining; consequently, some stores have closed.
9. Eve will be married next summer, and she and her husband will move to Phoenix.
10. Willy could scarcely lift the package; it was very heavy.
11. First you send for an application blank; then you get references.
12. We are rapidly exhausting some of our natural resources; for example, the oil supply is dwindling.
13. Most words have more than one meaning; therefore, you will need to use a dictionary.
14. You have seen this book before; it is now in paperback.
15. In the clear desert air, the mountains look very close; they are the Catalinas.

Page 376, Exercise C (Answers will vary.)

None of us could believe that Harry was guilty, for he had never been known to do anything dishonest. He had always been careful to give customers the exact change; yet, he was now charged with pilfering the cash register at his checkout counter. The manager himself usually picked up the extra cash twice a day. However, on Thursday he waited until the store closed. He put Harry's cash in a separate bag, and then he locked it up in the safe. When he counted it the next morning, it was ten dollars short. He accused Harry of pocketing the money; however, Harry denied the charge. He thought for a while, and then he asked to count the money. The manager agreed. He stood beside Harry while he counted. Harry went through each stack of bills slowly, and he found the ten dollars. Two ten-dollar bills had stuck together. The manager and his assistant apologized. They even let Harry pick up the cash from the checkout counters the next week to show that they trusted him.

Page 377, Review: Complete Sentences (Sentences will vary.)

1. The campers pitched their tent; they had found a perfect spot.
2. They hung provisions from a tree to prevent animals from getting the food.
3. Jeanne's favorite foods are spaghetti, steak, and ice cream that is dripping with chocolate sauce.
4. David was feeling happy about his high grades in math this semester.

5. Jon practices karate, and his sister is an instructor.
6. Lee has tickets to the Superbowl. It will be held in Miami.
7. I enjoyed the article that I read in *Rolling Stone* about Linda Ronstadt.
8. Would you like to appear on either a TV talk show or a game show?
9. Rosemary felt strange and lonely in her new school, which was very large.
10. The Lindsays have built an underground home because it will conserve heating energy.
11. Lillian Hellman, who wrote novels and plays, is the author of *Toys in the Attic.*
12. Drew was superstitious, and he always avoided the number thirteen.
13. Chris Evert began training as a tennis player when she was very young. Her father was her first coach.
14. Mr. and Mrs. Salido restore antique autos; then they display them at parades and fairs.
15. Kelp is a food source, and it is plentiful and nutritious.
16. Calligraphy is the art of handwriting.
17. Several schools are closing, for they have too few students.
18. During the last century, steamboats traveled the Mississippi River.
19. Robinson Crusoe is a famous literary character who was shipwrecked.
20. Having no permanent home, the workers followed the harvests; they lived in a bus.

Section 5
Agreement of Subject and Verb

Page 380, Exercise

1. were	8. are	15. want
2. was	9. was	16. look
3. Are	10. has	17. have
4. was	11. plans	18. Were
5. has	12. warm	19. is
6. is	13. works	20. has
7. comes	14. is	

Page 382, Exercise

1. suits	6. comes	11. was	16. carries
2. are	7. Has	12. know	17. is
3. has	8. was	13. seems	18. is
4. was	9. have	14. was	19. have
5. is	10. are	15. was	20. Has

Page 383, Exercise A

1. correct
2. The chairs and the table were loaded with packages.
3. Neither the gloves nor the sweater was the right size.
4. Either Cybil or Jeff has been here.
5. The gloves and the hat are the same color.
6. correct
7. Two books and a notebook are sitting on the desk.
8. The lifeguard or the swimming coach is always on duty.
9. Neither the newspapers nor the radio has reported the full story.
10. Either the meat or the potatoes are burning.

Page 384, Exercise B

1. Has either Mr. Barnes or Ms. Brown arrived yet?
2. Neither the doctor nor her nurse was at the office.
3. Two squirrels and a jackrabbit are all we saw.
4. correct
5. Neither the French fries nor the hamburger was hot.
6. Sandwiches or soup is your only choice.
7. correct
8. Neither the guard nor the police officer was really on the job.
9. Either Jack or his sister has your books.
10. Neither the audience nor the actors were aware of the trouble backstage.

Page 385, Exercise

1. Where's	6. are	11. Doesn't	16. is
2. Doesn't	7. were	12. are	17. pass
3. Here are	8. doesn't	13. There are	18. was
4. What are	9. are	14. go	19. Where are
5. were	10. moves	15. makes	20. What are

Page 388, Exercise

1. were	6. was	11. is	16. deals
2. were	7. is	12. was	17. is
3. is	8. was	13. was	18. was
4. is	9. want	14. sees	19. is
5. is	10. is	15. has	20. has

Page 390, Exercise A

1. have	5. are	8. calls
2. produce	6. listen	9. fall
3. is	7. is	10. march
4. has		

Page 390, Exercise B

1. aches	5. have	8. fail
2. resists	6. is	9. lasts
3. speaks	7. have	10. seems
4. has		

Page 391, Review: Agreement of Subject and Verb

1. is	6. makes	11. is	16. has
2. weighs	7. designs	12. are	17. is
3. has	8. struts	13. doesn't	18. is
4. use	9. are	14. sings	19. melts
5. expects	10. do	15. requires	20. are

Section 6
Pronoun Usage

Page 395, Exercise A

1. I	4. she	7. they	10. he	13. I
2. her	5. her	8. I	11. She	14. we
3. I	6. I	9. me	12. me	15. he

Page 396, Exercise B

1. him, me
2. them
3. her, him
4. them, us
5. they
6. we
7. me
8. them, us
9. me
10. he
11. she
12. he
13. she
14. me
15. them

Page 398, Exercise A

1. me
2. him
3. me
4. her
5. me
6. him
7. us
8. We
9. him
10. her, me
11. them, us
12. us
13. We
14. her
15. us

Page 398, Exercise B

1. her
2. me
3. us
4. she
5. me
6. him
7. us
8. me
9. We
10. she
11. we
12. me
13. us
14. me
15. him

Page 399, Exercise C

1. me
2. she, I
3. him, me
4. we
5. us
6. us
7. We
8. us
9. me
10. her
11. me
12. me
13. She, he
14. us
15. him, me
16. he
17. her
18. us
19. I
20. them

Page 400, Exercise

1. Who
2. Whom
3. Who
4. whom
5. whose
6. Whom
7. whose
8. who
9. Whom
10. Who
11. Whom
12. whom
13. Whom
14. Who
15. Whom

Page 402, Exercise

1. whose	6. whom	11. Whoever
2. who	7. who	12. who
3. whose	8. whomever	13. who
4. whoever	9. who	14. whom
5. who	10. who	15. whoever

Page 405, Exercise

1. I	6. she	11. ourselves	16. his
2. our	7. us	12. me	17. we
3. him	8. I	13. her	18. him
4. Their	9. her	14. me	19. him
5. him	10. they	15. you	20. they

Page 408, Exercise A

1. his, *or* his or her	6. are	11. Correct
2. he	7. his, *or* his or her	12. Correct
3. her	8. his	13. its
4. his, *or* his or her	9. he, *or* he or she	14. plan
5. Correct	10. his, *or* his or her	15. his, *or* his or her

Page 408, Exercise B

1. his, *or* his or her	5. you follow	9. his, *or* his or her
2. me	6. his, *or* his or her	10. his, *or* his or her
3. his, *or* his or her	7. he is, *or* he or she is	
4. we	8. he, *or* his or her	

Page 410, Exercise A (Sentences may vary somewhat.)

1. The article states that the President vetoed the bill.
2. Students write essays in English class.
3. He swung his racket but missed the ball.
4. During Prohibition, Congress made the sale of liquor illegal.
5. The tailor asked me to try the suit on.
6. The radio announcer said that the mayor has resigned.
7. Andy wants to become a chef because cooking interests him.

8. The best show that the educational station broadcasts is "Nova."
9. Students in this school are required to study a foreign language.
10. People who work in a laboratory are expected to be accurate.

Page 410, Exercise B (Sentences will vary somewhat.)

1. I missed Carl's birthday, and I'm sorry about my forgetfulness.
2. Maureen wants to be a ski instructor because the job is glamorous.
3. The exterior of the building is modern, but the interior is in ruins.
4. Visitors to Hawaii are greeted with flowers.
5. I have never told a lie, and my honesty once paid off.
6. Advertisements never tell the price.
7. Although the plumber worked hard, the faucet continued to leak.
8. Dropping temperatures may ruin the orange crop.
9. In Colonial days, the clergy preached very long sermons.
10. The supervisors at that job expect the employees to work long, hard hours.

Page 411, Exercise A (Sentences may vary somewhat.)

1. The candle broke when I put it in the holder.
2. To find out about his assignment, Jeff asked Mark.
3. Sara encouraged Tanya to try out for track.
4. The orange in this lunch bag isn't mine.
5. After she bought the plant, Alison put it in the wagon.
6. Before you wash the clothes, separate them from the towels.
7. Fred's car needed to be overhauled, Tom told him.
8. Katie's drawing won an award, Julie told her.
9. I put the money on the counter after taking it out of my wallet.
10. Dust the tennis rackets after you take them out of the presses.

Page 411, Exercise B (Sentences may vary somewhat.)

1. I can't find the magazine that I saw the picture in.
2. Joan washed her dress after removing the belt.
3. I always lose my notebooks, even though I keep them with my books.
4. Ellen had made a serious mistake, she told Kay.
5. The designer smiled as she talked to the model.
6. The traffic officer frowned as she spoke to Mom.
7. We can choose a different classroom or a different schedule if we want to make a change.
8. Put the groceries on the shelf after you take them out of the bags.

9. Uncle Kevin never pursued journalism, although he studied it in addition to acting.
10. The picture was too big to hang over the bookcase.

Page 412, Review: Pronoun Usage

1. They	6. Whom	11. the teachers	16. I
2. him	7. I	12. me	17. his
3. she	8. his	13. his or her	18. me
4. me	9. Whoever	14. her	19. it
5. We	10. me	15. her	20. who, his or her

Section 7

Adjective and Adverb Usage

Page 415, Exercise A

1. easily
2. unsteady
3. happy
4. steadily
5. rapidly
6. uneasy
7. quickly
8. certainly
9. different
10. badly

Page 415, Exercise B

1. nonstandard—You can get an office job more easily if you can take dictation.
2. nonstandard—Harriet seemed angry about the interruption.
3. nonstandard—You must drive more carefully.
4. standard
5. nonstandard—Barbara felt unhappy about her choice.
6. nonstandard—The repair shop fixed the radio perfectly.
7. standard
8. nonstandard—The old cottage on the dunes smelled damp.
9. nonstandard—We thought the dog was not behaving normally.
10. nonstandard—Herb studied the letter very carefully.

Page 417, Exercise

1. nonstandard—There are fewer pupils studying French this year.
2. standard
3. nonstandard—The milk tastes bad to me.
4. nonstandard—Be careful not to trip over those wires.
5. nonstandard—The bush grew well after being transplanted.
6. nonstandard—That kind of animal belongs in a zoo.
7. nonstandard—Secretaries should be able to spell well.
8. nonstandard—The team felt bad about Lindsay's injury.
9. standard
10. nonstandard—Fewer voters turned out than we had expected.
11. nonstandard—You can't buy that kind of candy any more.
12. nonstandard—Bob has all those power tools in his shop.
13. nonstandard—Mr. Jackson has looked bad ever since his operation.
14. standard
15. nonstandard—We had some of this kind of apple last year.
16. nonstandard—There have been fewer traffic deaths since we put in the new stoplight.
17. nonstandard—Leslie isn't singing as well as she did last week.
18. nonstandard—The boys were frightened badly by the runaway truck.
19. standard
20. nonstandard—The school chorus did very well in the regional contest.

Page 419, Exercise A (Sentence revisions may vary somewhat.)

1. Turn the radio up a little louder.
2. Our team is weaker this year because of minor injuries.
3. Some students can study more easily with the radio turned on.
4. Harry is the taller of the twins.
5. This was the least expensive coat of the dozen I looked at.
6. We watched both programs, but Alistair Cooke's was the better of the two.
7. Please open the window just a bit wider.
8. The water is softer now with the new filtration plant.
9. Our chances of winning are as good as theirs, if not better.
10. The problem is clearer to me now than before.

Page 420, Exercise B (Sentence revisions may vary somewhat.)

1. The work of a miner is more dangerous than that of a carpenter.
2. Joe is the smarter of that pair.
3. Joyce is as bright as any other member of the committee.

4. In the 1978 World Series, the Yankees had the better team.
5. Beth chose the longer of the two books for her report.
6. Please try to come over a little earlier than usual.
7. The coach was the best of the three speakers at the banquet.
8. I respect Betty Jean more than I do Chuck. (*or* I respect Betty Jean more than Chuck does.)
9. Our enrollment is bigger than ever this year.
10. Eve and Janet are both good students, but Janet is the better student.

Page 421, Exercise A (Sentence revisions may vary somewhat.)

1. The bus had never been so late before.
2. There had been nothing said about staying out of the water.
3. correct
4. Nobody in the audience could tell what had happened.
5. The doctor hasn't said anything that should frighten you.
6. By midnight the turkey had barely begun to thaw out.
7. Bob has none of his brother's charm.
8. correct
9. I'm sure that nobody else could have done as well.
10. We have had no response to our letter.

Page 421, Exercise B

1. You can easily finish the job in five minutes.
2. The roads are slippery. Drive carefully.
3. The papers had been stacked neatly on the desks.
4. Nomads have no homes. (*or* Nomads don't have any homes.)
5. Kris looked sadly at the empty cage.
6. You will have to speak a little more clearly.
7. In every pair of shoes, the right one is the bigger.
8. The score was much closer than in last year's game.
9. The class requested fewer assignments.
10. After the party there was hardly any food left.
11. We had peach pie and cherry pie, but the peach was better.
12. The victim's family took the news badly.
13. In a show of great football yesterday, the better team finally won.
14. Please don't order any more of those pencils.
15. correct
16. There were fewer cars on the road than we had expected.
17. The patient felt more grateful to the blood donor than to the doctors.
18. We stopped using that kind of helmet two years ago.
19. Be sure to clean the metal well before applying the enamel.
20. correct

Page 422, Review: Adjective and Adverb Usage

1. well	6. ever	11. fewer	16. foolish
2. bad	7. nervously	12. faster	17. anyone else
3. those	8. serious	13. any other	18. had
4. this	9. largest	14. any	19. easier
5. hardest	10. could	15. fewer	20. intently

Section 8

Verb Usage

Page 425, Exercise A

1. brought	6. fought	11. lent	16. flung
2. sat	7. fled	12. lost	17. led
3. got	8. flung	13. shone	18. shone
4. brought	9. dived or dove	14. stung	19. swung
5. caught	10. led	15. swung	20. lent

Page 425, Exercise B

1. brought	6. fled	11. flung	16. shone
2. caught	7. said	12. lent	17. stung
3. hurt	8. burst	13. led	18. shone
4. cost	9. stung	14. lent	19. swung
5. dived	10. fled	15. lost	20. caught

Page 427, Exercise A

1. borne	6. frozen	11. worn	16. broken
2. beaten	7. spoken	12. bore	17. chosen
3. bitten	8. stolen	13. borne	18. frozen
4. broken	9. sworn	14. beaten	19. torn
5. chosen	10. torn	15. bitten	20. worn

Page 427, Exercise B

1. worn	6. chosen	11. bore	16. stolen
2. sworn	7. broken	12. tore	17. tore
3. stolen	8. bitten	13. broken	18. beaten
4. spoken	9. broken	14. swore	19. bitten
5. frozen	10. beaten	15. frozen	20. spoken

Page 428, Exercise A

1. begun	6. sank or sunk	11. began	16. sang
2. drunk	7. rung	12. sang	17. rang
3. rang	8. sank or sunk	13. sank or sunk	18. swum
4. sung	9. sprang or sprung	14. drank	19. sunk
5. begun	10. swum	15. swam	20. sprung

Page 429, Exercise B

1. sang	6. drunk	11. began	16. swum
2. begun	7. rang	12. drunk	17. begun
3. sunk	8. sung	13. sprang or sprung	18. drank
4. sprang or sprung	9. sank or sunk	14. rang	19. rung
5. swam	10. sprung	15. drank	20. sang

Page 431, Exercise A

1. blew	6. eaten	11. known	16. taken
2. came	7. fallen	12. ridden	17. threw
3. done	8. gave	13. run	18. written
4. drew	9. gone	14. shook	19. written
5. driven	10. grew	15. slain	20. thrown

Page 431, Exercise B

1. blown	6. eaten	11. known	16. taken
2. come	7. fallen	12. ridden	17. thrown
3. did	8. gave	13. ran	18. done
4. drawn	9. gone	14. shaken	19. came
5. drove	10. grew	15. slain	20. seen

Page 432, Exercise C

1. blown
2. come
3. done
4. drawn
5. driven
6. eaten
7. fallen
8. gave
9. gone
10. grown
11. known
12. ridden
13. run
14. shook
15. taken
16. drawn
17. driven
18. fallen
19. given
20. grown

Page 434, Exercise A

1. lay
2. lain
3. laid
4. lay
5. lay
6. lying
7. lie
8. lain
9. laying
10. laid
11. lying
12. laid
13. lain
14. laid
15. lay
16. lying
17. laid
18. lie
19. laid
20. lying

Page 435, Exercise B

1. sitting
2. set
3. set
4. sitting
5. sit
6. set
7. set
8. sat
9. sitting
10. set
11. set
12. sitting
13. set
14. Sitting
15. set
16. sat
17. sitting
18. set
19. set
20. sitting

Page 436, Exercise C

1. risen
2. rise
3. risen
4. raised
5. raised
6. risen
7. rising
8. rising
9. raised
10. raised
11. raise
12. raise
13. raising
14. rose
15. raise
16. risen
17. raised
18. raise
19. risen
20. rose

Page 437, Review: Verb Usage

1. gone
2. cost
3. swung
4. hurt
5. sung
6. brought
7. bitten
8. broken
9. rung
10. shook
11. flung
12. beaten
13. drunk
14. known
15. lay
16. raised
17. lay
18. set
19. sat
20. raised

The Right Word

Page 441, Exercise A

1. After a lot of rest the patient is feeling all right.
2. Everyone except Monica has agreed on the new plan.
3. Did you bring back the rake I lent you?
4. Can you tell the difference between a peach and a nectarine?
5. Alligators differ from crocodiles in the shape of the snout.
6. I get angry at machines that don't return change.
7. The union members met all together and agreed among themselves on a strike.
8. An amendment to the Constitution must be adopted by three-fourths of the states.
9. May we go to the library?
10. A large number of students noticed the effect of soothing music in the cafeteria.

Page 441, Exercise B

1. The candidate has already agreed to a debate with her opponent.
2. The book I lent to Tom is nowhere to be found.
3. Heather adapted the story to suit the young listeners sitting beside her.
4. Now that I've accepted your advice, you're all ready to change your mind.
5. The weather can affect the number of people who vote.
6. Jet takeoffs disturb a lot of people who live beside the airport.
7. My counselor advised me to take a lot of math courses.
8. The two leaders disagreed between themselves on the issue of accepting the treaty.
9. Will you four girls please lift the mat all together and bring it toward me?
10. Environment affects a person's personality, but heredity also has an effect.

Page 445, Exercise A

1. The delegates must have spent most of the hour arguing.
2. An ice rink was formerly located beside the field house.
3. My parents let me choose which kind of bike to buy.
4. Has anyone really jumped off Niagara Falls?
5. Almost all of Poe's stories keep the reader in suspense.

6. Our coach taught us how to hit an overhead smash into the corner.
7. "That upset must have been an exciting game," Randi said.
8. Almost everyone felt as Liz did about the game, for there were a lot of unfair decisions.
9. Julia Child taught me how to make one kind of cake.
10. I infer from the judge's sentence that the murderer will be hanged.

Page 445, Exercise B

1. I wish our math teacher had let us leave class early.
2. Unfortunately, the first aid station was farther away than we had thought.
3. Almost everyone worries about falling off the catwalk, so it is seldom used.
4. The majority of motorcyle riders seldom used this sort of helmet.
5. A further goal of mine is to teach myself to play the guitar like James Taylor does.
6. Lavonne should have taken our advice and left her books in the car.
7. The horse looked sleek as it moved into the lead.
8. "Let me get up!" the boy shrieked, as if he had been attacked.
9. For the dance we hung colorful decorations from the ceiling.
10. The ambassador implied that he wanted to be formally invited to the reception.

Page 446, Review: The Right Word

1. May I help you take those books back to the library?
2. I wish we could have traveled somewhere in the South.
3. Will you lend me some kind of measuring stick?
4. Almost all of the contestants looked as if they might have been nervous.
5. Mr. Chang taught our class how reptiles differ from amphibians.
6. The sun is a lot farther from Earth than the moon is.
7. After we went into the building, Gilda hung her coat in her locker.
8. The coach wouldn't let us jump off the high dive.
9. Our hockey coach, who formerly played for the Blackhawks, seldom gives bad advice.
10. The principal has already agreed to a plan for changing the school's attendance policy.
11. I will accept any advice that sounds all right.
12. The counselor let Alicia and her parents decide among themselves.
13. Our teams have adopted another mascot besides the bulldog.
14. The conductor became angry with the musicians because they weren't playing all together.
15. In her speech, the commentator implied that most of the legal system was corrupt.

16. Weather affects the amount of crop yield that farmers get.
17. Anyway, Russia has a space program just as America does.
18. Most of the time the Royal Family does not dress formally.
19. The salesperson implied that there were only a certain number of tickets left.
20. The Senator differs with the President about the effect of inflation.

Section 10
Capitalization

Page 450, Exercise

1. How many German composers can you name?
2. The explorers skirted the Gulf of Mexico until they came to the Mississippi River.
3. There are not many English-speaking people in the Indonesian Republic.
4. Many of the Dutch speak German and English as well as their native tongue.
5. The Republic of Ghana lies on the west coast of Africa.
6. The Amazon River almost bisects the continent of South America.
7. In an old chest found in Death Valley, there was a copy of a New York newspaper.
8. The old Roman walls may still be seen in the northern parts of Great Britain.
9. The state of Minnesota is supposed to have 10,000 lakes.
10. For years, one part of the Western Plains was surrounded by Texas and Oklahoma, but it belonged to neither state.
11. You can now drive from New England to the Midwest on throughways.
12. Glacier National Park lies in the state of Montana.
13. Some people believe there is a difference between the American language and English.
14. Several languages are spoken in the Republic of the Philippines.
15. The geographic South Pole lies under a mass of ice in Antarctica.
16. Travelers can now go directly from the Jersey Turnpike to the Pennsylvania Turnpike.
17. The Ohio River forms part of the boundary of the state of Ohio.
18. The bus goes down Fifth Avenue to Washington Square.
19. Several American textbooks have been translated into Spanish for use in the schools of the Commonwealth of Puerto Rico.
20. There are still many Dutch ships steaming up the Hudson River.

Page 451, Exercise

1. Many factories from the North have moved into Southern states.
2. The people of the Southwest think of themselves as neither Southern nor Western.
3. Many Eastern students are going to Midwestern colleges.
4. correct
5. The Southeast and the Far West are the most rapidly growing sections of the country.
6. correct
7. correct
8. The civilization of the West has much to learn from that of the East.
9. There are many points at issue in East-West relations.
10. correct
11. Water shortage is becoming a serious problem in the Southeast.
12. The Northern papers were printing outrageous stories about the South, and Southern papers retaliated in kind.
13. From Manila, Dr. Robertson will fly west to the Middle East.
14. correct
15. We will take the northern route on our trip to the West.
16. The Western colleges are welcoming Eastern students.
17. The candidate for Vice-President will probably be a Westerner.
18. The birds fly south in September but return to the North in April.
19. correct
20. The Northern summer resorts attract many people from the South.

Page 453, Exercise

1. The Boston Choral Society will appear at the University of Maine.
2. The St. Louis Art Museum has a fine collection of Dutch paintings.
3. The Lerner String Quartet will play at the Library of Congress.
4. The New York Public Library has a fine collection of books on Buddhism.
5. Ship the English books to the Richmond Field High School.
6. The Hungarian people have an Asiatic background.
7. The Knights of Columbus have a new office near St. Mary's Hospital.
8. The Pennsylvania Railroad runs under the Hudson River into the Pennsylvania Station.
9. A friend of mine is teaching Spanish at Stanford University.
10. The Anglo-African Oil Company is not interested in aluminum.
11. My sister bought a secondhand Chevy van.
12. The summer school program offers English, chemistry, and American history.
13. Louis served us French toast with Vermont maple syrup.

14. The Junior Chamber of Commerce will campaign for a new hospital.
15. My mathematics teacher teaches Geometry II as well as Algebra I.
16. Where are the offices of the American Red Cross?
17. We bought our Sunspeed power mower at the Barclay Hardware Store.
18. Mr. Margolis works at the Morgan Guaranty Trust Company.
19. Our new offices are in the First National Bank building.
20. The new teacher is a leader in the Boy Scouts of America.

Page 455, Exercise

1. Aunt Rachel, Dad
2. ex-Governor Jones
3. Aunt Jenny, Colonel Hawkins, Governor
4. President-elect, Senators
5. *Rhapsody in Blue*
6. Cousin Bert
7. Officer Swenson
8. *A Raisin in the Sun*, Lorraine Hansberry
9. Doctor Pamela Payne
10. Henry Kissinger, Secretary of State, ex-President Ford
11. Justice Laura Larson
12. Governors, Secretary of the Interior
13. Mother, Father, Judge Krantz
14. Cousin Sandra, *Webster's New World Dictionary*
15. *Art Through the Ages*
16. *Two Years Before the Mast*
17. "The First Snowfall"
18. Chief of Police Johnson
19. Colonel Byrd, Lieutenant Wojack
20. Grandfather Brown

Page 457, Exercise A

1. Middle Ages
2. American, Age of Jackson
3. Declaration of Independence, Emancipation Proclamation
4. Battle of the Bulge, World War II
5. New York, Columbus Day
6. Prohibition Era
7. New Year's Eve
8. Convent of St. Paul the Apostle, Sisters of the Holy Ghost
9. Romantic Period, American
10. Second Continental Congress

Page 457, Exercise B

1. Vice-President, French Premier, National Airport
2. Social Security Act, Department of Health, Education, and Welfare
3. Captain Siple, Christmas, South Pole
4. Battle of Midway
5. Governor, Senator-elect
6. Congress, President Monroe, Monroe Doctrine
7. Ohio River, West
8. French, Midwest
9. Rocky Mountains
10. Irish, Dayton's Department Store, Fourth Street

Page 458, Review: Capitalization

1. Yes, Doctor Caldwell advised Mother to rest.
2. Yellowstone National Park is situated amid the Rocky Mountains.
3. Last Christmas Uncle Daniel gave me *Roots*.
4. Majorca is a Spanish island resort in the Mediterranean Sea.
5. The Orient has adopted many American customs.
6. Several Midwestern high schools are offering local history classes.
7. Do Brazilians speak Spanish or Portuguese?
8. The Gillette Company manufactures Toni hair care products.
9. The Gulf Stream keeps winters mild along Cape Cod.
10. During World War II Grandma worked at a munitions factory.
11. At Poppin' Fresh I had the Dutch apple pie with Swiss cheese.
12. The Greyhound bus traveled north along the Edens Expressway.
13. In July, Britain's Prince Charles will visit Boston and Hartford.
14. One reporter asked Representative Simms and Senator Pasquale for reports of their earnings.
15. Great Britain's Prime Minister visited Washington, D.C., last fall.
16. At Stevenson High School, Advanced Algebra II begins with a review of Algebra I.
17. Headquarters for the United Nations are in New York City.
18. "Who were the world rulers," Ms. Ellman asked, "in 100 B.C.?"
19. Reciting verses from the *Bible*, the Pilgrims celebrated the first Thanksgiving Day.
20. Following the Civil War, the Reconstruction Acts restored the Southern states to Congress.

Section 11

End Marks and Commas

Page 460, Exercise A

1. At what time does the game begin?
2. Mr. L. V. Costello left his office at 4:30 P.M.
3. I've been robbed!
4. Does the plane from Omaha arrive at 4:10 A.M. or 4:10 P.M.?
5. Have you ever watched "Marcus Welby, M.D."?
6. Gov. Ella Grasso has served in Congress.
7. Emily Ray, D.D.S., used to work for General Foods, Inc.
8. Dr. J. A. Larson, Jr. will attend a conference in Washington, D.C.
9. The contract was arranged between Brightons, Ltd. of England and Sweetways, Inc. of New York.
10. Who ruled the Mediterranean world from 100 B.C. to A.D. 200?

Page 461, Exercise B

1. Don't touch that wire!
2. When the box arrives, may we open it?
3. The book was written by the Reverend Thomas Powers, S.J.
4. Susan B. Anthony was a leader in the women's suffrage movement, wasn't she?
5. Help! The rug is on fire!
6. Brig. Gen. M. E. Clark is director of the Women's Army Corps.
7. Did Dr. Martin Luther King , Jr. win the Nobel peace prize in 1963 or 1964?
8. Does the IRS check up on the FBI?
9. The meeting was addressed by Asst. Dep. José Rivera.
10. Professor Marilyn Bernard, D. Sc. was appointed to the ICC.

Page 462, Exercise A

1. Honestly, we are not justified in complaining.
2. At the start of the campaign, Ms. Anson was favored to win.
3. Well, no one was more surprised at the outcome than Robbie.
4. If possible, make the appointment for Wednesday.
5. correct
6. After scoring six runs in the first inning, the Mets let up.
7. To avoid excess nervous tension, practice physical relaxation.

8. Counting on surprise strategy, Greenville passed on the first down.
9. correct
10. Although the road was icy, we made fairly good time.

Page 462, Exercise B

1. No, there is no other way out of the valley.
2. When Mozart was six, he was performing his music in the courts of Europe.
3. Concentrating intensely, Lynn went over her report again.
4. Yes, Amelia Earhart was the first woman to fly solo across the ocean.
5. Dropping their tools, the workers scrambled for safety.
6. correct
7. When the tide went out, we walked along the sandy beach.
8. correct
9. Hard as she worked, the younger child could not catch up to the rest of the class.
10. Why, no one warned us to shut off the water.

Page 465, Exercise A

1. We visited the Adams Library, one of the oldest in America.
2. There is no doubt, my friends, that we have hard times ahead of us.
3. One field of science, computer technology, is almost completely devoted to storing and transmitting information.
4. The damage, however, was less than we had expected.
5. A completely honest person, I can assure you, is hard to find.
6. Your second sentence, for example, is much too long.
7. The door was opened by the butler, a tall man with brooding eyes.
8. The game was played, as a matter of fact, exactly as we had planned it.
9. Therefore, the library will be closed on Saturday.
10. The company has moved its offices to Morristown, New Jersey.

Page 465, Exercise B

1. Reno, Nevada, lies farther west than Los Angeles, California.
2. Our new address is 41 East Twelfth Street, New York, New York 10003.
3. The treaty was signed in Geneva, Switzerland, on December 15, 1906, but it was not ratified until March 6, 1908.
4. On July 5, 1835, there were snowstorms in New England.

5. Lee was born in Evanston, Illinois, on December 19, 1965.
6. You know, my colleagues, we may be on the verge of a revolution in printing.
7. This house, as you can see, was built on a rocky ledge.
8. We will meet you at Canton, Ohio, on Wednesday, January 10.
9. The entrapped miners decided, therefore, to make one more try.
10. It is up to you, my friends, to decide what kind of society you want to live in.

Page 467, Exercise

1. restrictive
2. nonrestrictive—Standing in the doorway, Drew asked if he could come in.
3. restrictive
4. nonrestrictive—Mr. Salvatore, who is a famous singer, will train our class.
5. nonrestrictive—The Carlsbad Caverns, which attract sightseers to New Mexico, are the largest known underground caverns.
6. nonrestrictive—The train, struck by the avalanche, was tossed down the hillside.
7. restrictive
8. restrictive
9. nonrestrictive—The new toll road, which will be opened Friday, will save us a great deal of time.
10. nonrestrictive—Mom's office, which has always been dark, has been redecorated.
11. nonrestrictive—The new show, which was highly praised by reviewers, was a disappointment to us.
12. restrictive
13. nonrestrictive—We waited until the last moment, hoping you would appear.
14. restrictive
15. restrictive
16. nonrestrictive—Our neighbor, who is a fine mechanic, helped us repair the dishwasher.
17. restrictive
18. nonrestrictive—The coach, fearing overconfidence, put the team through a hard drill.
19. restrictive
20. nonrestrictive—The room, which was too small in the first place, was now overcrowded.

Page 470, Exercise

1. We asked Marion to come with us, but she had another engagement.
2. The lights, the movements, and the presents make a pretty picture.
3. We had not intended to stay overnight, but the snowfall turned into a blizzard.
4. The officer asked for Bob's license, looked it over, and got out her notebook.
5. The doctor must come soon, or he will be too late.
6. Beethoven wrote symphonies, quartets, concertos, and sonatas.
7. Three trucks, four cars, and a trailer were tangled on the icy bridge.
8. Luanne found the geology course interesting, practical, but difficult.
9. The boss frowned, tried to look severe, and finally grinned.
10. The entire roll of film was either blurred, dark, or out of focus.
11. Harry has his pass, but he cannot leave the base until tomorrow.
12. Helen entered the room, walked straight to the table, and called the meeting to order.
13. Strange noises were coming from the stereo, from the water pipes, and from the attic.
14. I could not reach the top shelf, nor could I find the stepladder.
15. You had better start now, or you will miss the last bus.
16. Couples were standing in the streets, sitting on telephone poles, and leaning out of windows.
17. A flight attendant must be cheerful, alert, and always pleasant.
18. We had expected to arrive by midnight, but the plane could not land.
19. All roads, bridges, and highways into the city have been closed by the heavy snowstorm.
20. Suddenly, the commanding officer picked up a pen, reached for my papers, signed them, and tossed them across the desk to me.

Page 472, Exercise A

1. Ms. Ellis sent four letters; Ms. Harris, two dozen postcards.
2. I recognized none of the group, but Todd had known one of the boys in summer camp.
3. Once before, the stage curtain had stuck halfway up.
4. After cooking, Roger cleaned up the kitchen.
5. Amy wore red socks; Melinda, blue ones.
6. Luis tasted all the pies, but one was too hot.
7. To play, a stereo must have speakers.
8. Inside, the house smelled of freshly baked brownies.
9. From calling, Ben lost his voice.
10. Beyond, the residential section extends for ten miles.

Page 472, Exercise B

1. Inside, the church was beautifully lighted.
2. Above, the men were dangling ropes over the cliff.
3. Before leaving, the janitor locked the windows.
4. As he wrote, the short story became very long.
5. Underneath, the boat was covered with slime.
6. John Steinbeck wrote *Of Mice and Men*; Leonard Wibberly, *The Mouse that Roared*.
7. When a doctor is called, to cure a patient is his or her aim.
8. All the girls went to the game, but Sue had to babysit.
9. Skip set out the chairs on the porch, for the guests were arriving.
10. Outside, the house looked as though no one lived there.

Page 473, Review: End Marks and Commas

1. Fortunately, Yoshi is much healthier now.
2. Hooray! Our team made the finals!
3. Both of my sisters are successful salespersons, but the one that sells cars is Angela.
4. When the movie is over, will you pick us up?
5. Scanning the area, the forest ranger noticed a distant cloud of smoke.
6. Well, leap year, of course, has an extra day.
7. Settlers landed at Salem, Massachusetts, on September 6, 1628.
8. After calling, Tina let her brother use the phone.
9. J. Edgar Hoover, I believe, was head of the FBI for many years.
10. April Fool's Day, a day for harmless pranks and jokes, is observed on April 1.
11. My uncle, trying to lose weight, eats a lot of salads, fruit, and cottage cheese.
12. Ms. Hansen, did you travel to Paris, or did you stay in London?
13. The time in San Diego is 9 A.M.; in Baltimore, 12 noon.
14. The northern kit fox, which is native to Canada, is an endangered species.
15. The East Building of the National Galley of Art in Washington, D.C., was designed by I. M. Pei.
16. Traveling through outer space, the astronaut radioed to Earth.
17. Undoubtedly, Dr. Sayner, who is the team doctor, will tape your ankle.
18. Yes, please send my T-shirt to 383 Picardy Lane, Rome, New York.
19. Nautilus, the first atomic submarine, was launched on January 21, 1954.
20. Wow! If the experts are correct, Karen, we will soon have computerized homes.

Section 12

The Semicolon, the Colon, the Dash, and Parentheses

Page 476, Exercise

1. We are disappointed in the advertisement; it is too small.
2. The team went to the hospital to see Bud; he had been hurt in Saturday's game.
3. Sylvia is doing very well; in fact, she has a B+ average.
4. Dictionaries do not always agree; for instance, they differ on the pronunciation of *duty*.
5. correct
6. We have a factory in Salem, Ohio; an office in Buffalo, New York; and a mill at Andover, Massachusetts.
7. Dave Rotnam won first prize; his sister Joan, second prize; and Davina Belknap, third prize.
8. Eve was surrounded by notebooks, encyclopedias, and dictionaries; but she was reading a letter from Bill.
9. correct
10. For Christmas, I got a radio; Mark, a typewriter; and Inez, a new suit.
11. We ought to beat Hinsdale, Elmhurst, and Bensenville; but we may lose to Oak Park.
12. The building was designed by Frank Lloyd Wright, the famous American architect; but the New York critics, in their newspaper columns, attacked it savagely.
13. The electricity was off for six hours; consequently, everything in our food locker was spoiled.
14. Ms. Novicki has been on the force for twenty-three years; she is almost ready to retire.
15. Ellen has a new camera; it was made in Germany.

Page 479, Exercise

1. Beginning next January we shall handle the following foreign cars: Datsun, Volvo, Volkswagen, and Honda.
2. The candidate's main qualifications were these: twelve years' experience in the Senate, a knowledge of foreign affairs, and the ability to get votes.
3. I am looking for the source of this quotation: "Always do right. This will gratify some people and astonish the rest."

4. Our new text is called *Supershopper: A Guide to Spending and Saving*.
5. The quotation is found in *The Oxford English Dictionary*, Vol. II: page 427.
6. High school students today are more serious; they expect to work hard.
7. Alice knew—at least she thought she knew—what was coming next.
8. It is our obligation—there is no choice in the matter—to pay all of Frank's expenses to the convention.
9. It's about—well, it's something like—I would say it's a good ten miles from here.
10. Having a lot of clothes, owning a fancy car, going to parties—are these really suitable goals in life?
11. The prizes are as follows: first prize, a movie camera; second prize, a portable TV set; third prize, a pocket-size calculator.
12. You have three jobs for today: wash the car, clean up the yard, and shop for your mother.
13. The President closed with these words: "With God's help, we can face the future hopefully, in full confidence that our problems can be solved."
14. Marion saw the point; no one else did.
15. We shall cover the following topics in this conference: planning for new products, improving customer relations, and marketing.
16. You will find the statement in *Thomas Jefferson: The Man and His Times*, Volume III: page 106.
17. You can take this road down—but I guess the road is closed, isn't it?
18. There is a strange light—a reddish light that moves very fast—in the sky to the south of here.
19. All of a sudden—we had already closed the door—the telephone began ringing.
20. It is rather a long walk; however, it is a pleasant one.

Page 481, Review: The Semicolon, the Colon, the Dash, and Parentheses

1. Evan uses a calculator; Lettie uses a slide rule.
2. Educational television has many good shows; for instance, I enjoy "Once upon a Classic."
3. The horse ran, pranced, and galloped; but then he needed a rest.
4. The following magazines have the highest circulation: *Reader's Digest*, *Parade*, and *TV Guide*.
5. The librarian advised me to check Volume 4: pages 101–150.
6. Panting, the marathon runner crossed the finish line; she had come in first.

7. Our school has exchange students from these countries: Brazil, Kenya, Sweden, and Chile.
8. Costumes, scrapbooks, toys, and dishes—we found them all in the attic.
9. I guessed the trial's outcome: The accused murderer would be found guilty.
10. The water ballet routine was precisely choreographed; furthermore, it was performed flawlessly.
11. My class that meets at 9:30—oh, I hope I won't be late—will discuss student rights.
12. Alana is the editor-in-chief of the school newspaper; Janie, the business manager; and Reggie, the staff photographer.
13. The Declaration of Independence ends with these words: "We mutually pledge to each other our lives, our fortunes, and our sacred honor."
14. The coach tried everything—pep talks, privileges, rallies, toughness—to try to improve the team's morale.
15. *Newsweek* magazine (*Time's* chief competitor) features a guest essay called "My Turn."
16. Spiders, ants, fleas, roaches—they're all part of my insect collection.
17. The following cities have warm winters: Miami, Florida; Los Angeles, California; and Honolulu, Hawaii.
18. Ms. Conti, do you have *JFK: The Early Years*, or has it been checked out?
19. Selina prepared for the audition: She memorized her lines and practiced her dance.
20. There are many calendars; for example, ancient Romans used the Julian calendar.

Section 13
The Apostrophe

Page 484, Exercise

1. girls'	6. passengers'	11. reporters'	16. correct
2. correct	7. correct	12. clients'	17. correct
3. Tom's	8. correct	13. correct	18. President's
4. girl's	9. correct	14. sailors'	19. correct
5. correct	10. teachers'	15. actors'	20. women's

Page 487, Exercise

1. sister-in-law's
2. Dana's and Paul's
3. anybody's
4. weeks'
5. Smith and Weston's
6. days'
7. Roger and Sons'
8. Roosevelt's and Rockefeller's
9. hours'
10. League of Women Voters'
11. hour's, day's
12. Chase and Maxwell's
13. somebody else's
14. Secretary of the Treasury's
15. mothers' and sons'
16. Lord and Taylor's
17. Andy and Marge's
18. months'
19. Benét's and Twain's
20. moment's

Page 488, Exercise A

1. There are too many *that*'s in your sentence.
2. Perry's address has four 3's in it.
3. There should be great prosperity in the 1980's.
4. It was three o'clock before we got started.
5. It's not likely that Mars or Venus is inhabited.
6. We don't know the answer to the question, and we can't find it.
7. It is clear now that Dad's letter won't come today.
8. Jess's short story is being published in *Scholastic Magazine*.
9. Our local paper's feature section gives career tips.
10. We don't yet know who's coming.
11. Is there a good men's store in town?
12. The flight attendants' smiles were reassuring when the plane began to bounce.
13. The county's highway department is in charge of snow removal.
14. The waitresses' hours and wages are good at Barney's Restaurant.
15. By working overtime, we earned a week's wages in two days' time.
16. You can buy women's coats in the young ladies' department.
17. Ward was always too interested in everyone else's business.
18. Have you ever shopped at a farmer s'market?
19. Charles's order must have been lost in the mail.
20. The tugs' whistles set up a frightful clamor in the harbor.

Page 489, Exercise B

1. woman's   women's
2. man's   men's
3. class's   classes'
4. salesperson's   salespersons'
5. hour's   hours'
6. lady's   ladies'
7. fox's   foxes'
8. city's   cities'

9. boss's	bosses'	13. company's	companies'
10. employee's	employees'	14. mouse's	mice's
11. day's	days'	15. bus's	buses'
12. dollar's	dollars'		

Page 489, Exercise C

1. There is a new boys' camp across the lake.
2. Do you have an account at James and Law's store?
3. Mosquitoes find me very appealing, don't they?
4. The editor-in-chief's editorial criticized the cafeteria's food.
5. Pat and Gladys's telephone conversation went on for hours.
6. Juanita is working at Harris and Sons' store in Milwaukee.
7. Diana Ross and the Supremes' records will never be equaled.
8. We are publishing a collection of the year's best sports stories.
9. The girls' locker room was built by the town's best carpenter.
10. Mr. Garvey's car won't be ready until Friday.
11. What is your father-in-law's business?
12. It's too late to go to Bobby Holmes's party.
13. Everyone else's boat was damaged in the storm.
14. My typewriter's keys stick on the *e*'s.
15. Ms. Smith's glasses are in someone's car.
16. The speaker's lecture could not be heard above the audience's coughing.
17. The Farewell Address was both Hamilton's and Washington's work.
18. Ross's friend has just bought the J. C. Little and Company's building.
19. Two weeks' stay here will give you a year's good health.
20. Mason and Dixon's survey settled many territorial disputes.

Page 490, Review: The Apostrophe

1. Bross and Brady's Gourmet Shop sells pickled eel.
2. Several golfers' scores were below par.
3. Doesn't the women's locker room have a sauna?
4. It would take two weeks' work to get Kelly's room clean.
5. The child gleefully turned the jack-in-the-box's handle.
6. Alison's phone number has four 8's in a row.
7. This year's football squad isn't strong on defense.
8. Druid and Company's policy is never to hire teen-agers.
9. No one's jeans look as new as Terry's.
10. The treasurer of the class of '84 must collect each member's fees.
11. You'll have to borrow someone else's class notes, José.
12. A bird sheds its feathers during molting season.

13. Katie and Les's project demonstrates how heredity determines the color of our eyes.
14. Foxes' and minks' furs are used for coats, aren't they?
15. This seminar is supposed to teach the ABC's of ecology in the 1980's.
16. Their club's skit is a parody of *The Wiz*.
17. The baseball is Adam's, but the bat is hers.
18. During a speech, too many *um*'s are distracting.
19. Mr. Moran's and Ms. Sax's classes are visiting the space museum.
20. Can't you recognize the lilies-of-the-valley's fragrance?

Section 14
Quotations

Page 491, Exercise

1. direct—"The test was hard," said Sam, "but it was fair."
2. indirect
3. direct—"May I have a new shirt for the party?" asked Ken.
4. indirect
5. indirect
6. direct—"No one would think to look in here," said Ms. Brown.
7. direct—Ben called out, "We will be home early."
8. direct—"The city is not equipped to deal with a heavy snowfall," the guide explained.
9. direct—"Does anyone know," asked Loretta, "who is to be the speaker at the assembly?"
10. direct—"Well, I think I left it on the bus, but I may have left it in the store," said Jean sadly.

Page 494, Exercise A

1. Molly asked, "Does anyone remember when the book reports are due?"
2. "We can't decide," Mother said, "whether to paint the house or buy a new car."
3. Zachary asked, "May I rewrite this paper?"
4. "There is no excuse for this delay," said the customer. "We gave you our order two months ago."
5. "Your Honor," the defendant pleaded, "I beg you for another chance."

6. "In the Sand Creek Massacre," the speaker added, "several hundred Indians were killed."
7. Did Captain Perry's message say, "We have met the enemy and they are ours"?
8. "Look out for a pass!" Bill shouted.
9. "Did you finish your homework?" Sarah asked.
10. "Do you happen to know," asked Jack, "where we can get another tire?"

Page 494, Exercise B

1. "Are you absolutely sure," Burt asked, "that the water has been turned off?"
2. "What can we do now?" asked Beth. "Our money is all gone."
3. Dave replied, "I am sure the officer said to drive on through."
4. "You can be sure," Mark promised, "that we will not forget your kindness."
5. "Is it too late to apply for a job?" asked Jeff.
6. "I am not afraid of the dark," said Harold, "but I'm not afraid of a little light either."
7. "Watch out!" Marta yelled. "Isn't that a snake by your foot?"
8. Did you hear the coach say, "No new plays this week"?
9. "Do you have my pen?" asked Kathy. "I will need it."
10. "Did the referee say 'strike three'?" Rita asked.

Page 496, Exercise A

1. What does the word *serendipity* mean?
2. There are too many *and*'s in your sentences.
3. Read Phyllis McGinley's poem "Reflections Dental."
4. The hardest words on the vocabulary test were *quay* and *spurn*.
5. There is an interesting article entitled "Swimming with Right Whales" in this month's *National Geographic*.
6. Doris always has a hard time spelling *recommend*.
7. The British word for *elevator* is *lift*.
8. Rachel will lead a discussion of the story "The Open Boat."
9. *Epilog* means "a concluding part added to a literary work."
10. Helen Reddy's most popular song was "I Am Woman."

Page 496, Exercise B

1. In Canada the word is spelled *colour*.
2. "Mother to Son" is my favorite poem in the book *Literature Lives*.

3. Todd calls money "bread," and Meg calls it "the green stuff."
4. Read the chapter called "Bacteria Are Your Friends."
5. Why are those islands called "The Lesser Antilles"?
6. John Denver describes nearly everything as "far out."
7. Katie cringes when anyone calls her "honey" or "sweetie."
8. What is meant by the phrase "manifest destiny"?
9. Would the chef call this meal a "gourmet great"?
10. How are you using the word *break* in the sentence beginning with *Thieves?*

Page 497, Review: Quotations

1. "I'll be a few minutes late," Johanna remarked.
2. After the feast Bob asked, "Did you get enough to eat?"
3. "I give up," said Phil. "What is the answer?"
4. Jenina complained that getting up early was a "bummer."
5. The consumer expert began her report, "Commercials can make us dissatisfied."
6. "I did it!" the contest winner shouted.
7. One chapter of *The Martian Chronicles* is called "The Green Morning."
8. We read O. Henry's story "The Ransom of Red Chief."
9. Sabrina asked, "Did you read the poem 'Fifteen'?"
10. The TV term for an added sound track of people laughing is "canned laughter."
11. The word *madam* is spelled the same forwards and backwards.
12. "Thanks to television," Fred Allen said, "the next generation will have four eyes and no tongue."
13. Our English teacher said that *genre* means "a kind or type of artistic endeavor."
14. Carla asked, "Did Mr. Oldfield say, 'Class is dismissed'?"
15. Why do TV emcees say, "We'll be back after this word from our sponsor"?
16. "Who wrote the book *The Long Winter?*" Vivienne asked.
17. "Whoopee!" the announcer shouted. "The Rangers have won!"
18. "Ms. Armada, does the word *subsequent* mean 'next'?" Sonia asked.
19. "The following states," explained Ralph, "are the only ones we have ever visited: Texas, Florida, Georgia, and Arizona.
20. "Sherlock Holmes remarks, 'Elementary, my dear Watson,' in many of the stories," Nicole notes.

Section 15
Spelling

Page 499, Exercise (Word divisions may vary.)

1. oc-cur-rence
2. ac-ci-den-tal-ly
3. ac-com-mo-date
4. in-cred-i-ble
5. mis-cel-la-ne-ous
6. main-te-nance
7. hu-mor-ous
8. spe-cif-i-cal-ly
9. nec-es-sar-y
10. dis-ap-pear-ance
11. mim-e-o-graph
12. im-me-di-ate-ly
13. i-tal-i-cize
14. min-i-a-ture
15. ex-tra-or-di-nar-y
16. sec-re-tar-i-al
17. ath-let-ic
18. priv-i-lege

Page 500, Exercise A

1. lazily
2. invitation, famous
3. architectural, admirable
4. courageous
5. noticeable
6. moving, icy
7. guidance
8. arguments, immovable
9. wholly
10. incredibly
11. lonely, lonelier
12. craziest, imaginable
13. continuing, intensive
14. arrival, usually
15. sixtieth, merriment
16. haziness
17. heavier, immovable
18. earliest, easily
19. likable, exciting
20. clumsily, fortifications

Page 501, Exercise B

1. mysterious
2. relaying
3. bodily
4. frenzied
5. appraised
6. wasteful
7. amazing
8. insurance
9. greasy
10. situation
11. worrying
12. carried
13. enjoyable
14. creative
15. copying
16. education
17. assemblage
18. widely
19. constitution
20. likable
21. movement
22. changeable
23. charging
24. hurrying
25. debatable
26. hastily
27. merrily
28. easily
29. daily
30. argument

Page 502, Exercise A

1. thinness
2. dissatisfied
3. greenness
4. usually
5. irresponsible
6. unevenness
7. preceded
8. surely
9. recommend, extremely
10. Finally, disappeared
11. immaterial, irrelevant
12. Naturally, disappointed
13. correct
14. gracefully, succeeded
15. immobile, coolly
16. illegal, immoral
17. proceeded, carefully
18. Actually, preceded
19. unnecessary, exceed
20. conceded, eventually

Page 503, Exercise B

1. thinness
2. misstate
3. irrelevant
4. immoderate
5. dissatisfied
6. cooperate
7. incidentally
8. immobilize
9. unevenness
10. immoral
11. confidentially
12. reexamine
13. disappear
14. cordially
15. disagree

Page 503, Exercise A

1. piece, brief
2. priest, shielded
3. tier
4. reprieve
5. chief, shield
6. believe, yield
7. niece, receipt
8. perceive, ceiling
9. field
10. Neither, leisure
11. deceit
12. wielded
13. believe
14. relieved
15. conceive, weird
16. shriek, pierced
17. brief, handkerchief
18. chief, piece
19. pier, retrieved
20. perceived

Page 504, Exercise B

1. perceive
2. neither
3. ceiling
4. receipt
5. chief
6. fierce
7. niece
8. shield
9. seize
10. piece
11. grievance
12. hygiene
13. pier
14. thief
15. leisure

Page 505, Exercise A

1. control'
2. excel'
3. lim'it
4. resist'
5. omit'
6. regret'
7. allot'
8. impel'
9. trav'el
10. distill'
11. forget'
12. mur'mur
13. defer'
14 ben'efit
15. admit'
16. dif'fer
17. infer'
18. propel'
19. submit'
20. begin'

Page 506, Exercise B

1. controlling
2. batted
3. compelled
4. bedding
5. difference
6. limited
7. committed
8. booked
9. furry
10. disappeared
11. putting
12. getting
13. planning
14. preferred
15. sitting
16. remittance
17. transferring
18. nodding
19. beginning
20. expelled
21. admittance
22. letting
23. padded
24. murmuring
25. repelled
26. omitted
27. committed
28. tonnage
29. allotted
30. deferred

Page 507, Exercise

1. dessert
2. desert
3. its
4. It's
5. there
6. their
7. They're
8. whether
9. weather
10. Who's
11. Whose
12. your
13. you're
14. lose
15. loose
16. principles
17. principal
18. to
19. too
20. stationary

Page 512, Review: Spelling

1. field, carefully
2. Raking, believe
3. truly, courageous
4. Writing, precisely, copied
5. usually, disapproves
6. proceeded, its, desert
7. clapped, appeared
8. excelled, inferences
9. your, whose
10. busiest
11. suspenseful, illegal
12. correct
13. weird, recurred, answered
14. perceived, stationary
15. generally, companies
16. whether
17. happily, gracefully
18. argument, inappropriate, here
19. dessert, piece, creamy, too
20. coordination, evenness

Section 16
The Plurals of Nouns

Page 516, Exercise A

1. holidays
2. herds
3. glasses
4. radios
5. dashes
6. heroes
7. watches
8. laboratories
9. ladies
10. cupfuls
11. studios
12. counties
13. valleys
14. beliefs
15. potatoes
16. handkerchiefs
17. griefs
18. hypotheses
19. data
20. bases
21. tablespoonfuls
22. fathers-in-law
23. drive-ins
24. attorneys-general
25. rights of way
26. chiefs of police
27. clerks of court
28. Supreme Court Justices
29. bills of sale
30. notaries public

Page 516, Exercise B

1. data
2. hypotheses
3. brothers-in-law
4. cupfuls
5. leaves
6. potatoes, tomatoes
7. sopranos
8. studios
9. Marches, Lyonses
10. catches
11. countries
12. mothers-in-law
13. countries, parties
14. autos, cities
15. duties, phenomena
16. Chinese
17. notaries public
18. armfuls
19. moose
20. sheep, wolves
21. heroes, lives
22. hangers-on, parties
23. boxes, matches
24. thieves, brothers-in-law
25. knives, gashes

Page 517, Review: The Plurals of Nouns

1. desks
2. crutches
3. paradoxes
4. convoys
5. opportunities
6. tomatoes
7. echoes
8. altos
9. radios
10. selves
11. loaves
12. chefs
13. freshmen
14. moose
15. crises
16. Barneses
17. handfuls
18. bookcases
19. sisters-in-law
20. editors-in-chief

Section 17

Good Manuscript Form

Page 521, Exercise

1. correct
2. Seven of the students in my class worked on the float for the parade.
3. When we arrived in Duluth, it was 20 degrees below zero.
4. correct
5. Nearly 60 percent of high school graduates now go on to college.
6. The offices are now located at 1741 Broadway.
7. The satellite whirled about the earth every $4\frac{3}{10}$ minutes.
8. correct
9. Our room number is 426.
10. correct
11. The telephone number here is 275-4000.
12. The date on the flyleaf was 1897.
13. Helen's new address is 220 East End Avenue.
14. We have room for only seven hundred students in the college.
15. More than five hundred students are singing in the all-state chorus.

Page 523, Exercise

1. The Reverend Carol Anderson, D.D., is one of the speakers.
2. Your reservation is on American Airlines for next Saturday.
3. Twelve-year-old Pam is the youngest student at Mather High School.
4. The Hershey Company is located in Hershey, Pennsylvania.
5. For twenty-three days during August, Anita will be traveling in Ireland.
6. Mr. Walsh and James Perrin are at a convention in Denver, Colorado.
7. Bob has an appointment with Dr. Kim at 4:00 P.M. on Friday.
8. Ms. Marks has just been made vice-president of the bank.
9. The long-awaited Christmas vacation will start on December 21.
10. Our biology assignment is to read pages 46 to 62.
11. The well-meaning club secretary has very little to do.
12. We used to live in Illinois, but then we moved to Michigan.
13. The doctor delivered a baby that weighed seven pounds eight ounces.
14. Augustus ruled the Roman Empire from 27 B.C. to A.D. 14.
15. In northern Minnesota, I once caught a pike sixteen inches long.

Page 528, Review: Good Manuscript Form

1. The play-offs are between Clemente High School and Loyola Academy.

2. That fifteen minute phone call cost $5.12, Dr. Kowinski.
3. Dial 936-1212 for the National Weather Service forecast.
4. A kilogram equals 2.2 pounds, and a gram equals .035 ounces.
5. According to a writer in *The New York Times*, the word *lifestyle* is being overused.
6. Twenty-four well-qualified students were elected to Student Association.
7. St. Patrick's Day is celebrated on March 17.
8. The Parent Teachers Association has its headquarters at 700 North Rush Street, Chicago, Illinois.
9. The chart on page 60 of *Modern Biology* explains the classification of vertebrates.
10. Canada is divided into ten provinces, just as the United States is divided into fifty states.
11. The largest lake in the world is the Caspian Sea with an area of 143,550 square miles.
12. The President's appointments secretary declined three-fourths of the invitations.
13. About 75 percent of all active volcanoes are located in an area called the "Ring of Fire."
14. The ocean liner *Queen Elizabeth* weighed 83,673 tons.
15. Birgitta has that all-knowing attitude that some people call *savoir-faire*.
16. Sixty thousand people attended the all-star benefit performance at Madison Square Garden.
17. The Osmonds are a close-knit family.
18. Britishers use the word "petrol" when they refer to gasoline.
19. Is the *St. Louis Post-Dispatch* a pro-Republican newspaper?
20. In all states but four, women may marry at age eighteen without consent of their parents.

Section 18

Outlining

Page 534, Exercise Note: Some items of the same rank, such as D and E under III, are interchangeable.

First Steps to First Aid

First aid techniques can provide emergency treatment until medical help arrives.

I. Goals of first aid
   A. To ease pain
   B. To prevent worsening
   C. To soothe fears
II. General techniques of first aid
   A. Staying calm
   B. Avoiding movement of victim
   C. Examining the victim
      1. For burns
      2. For cuts or wounds
      3. For fractures
   D. Reassuring the victim
   E. Preventing shock
      1. Symptoms of shock
      2. Treatment of shock
         a. Covers
         b. Hot drinks
III. Situations requiring first aid
   A. Animal bites
   B. Severe bleeding
   C. Asphyxiation
   D. Frostbite
   E. Fractures
   F. Fainting
   G. Heatstroke
   H. Burns
   I. Poisoning
   J. Severe cuts

Page 536, Review: Outlining Note: Some items of the same rank, such as 1 and 2 under A, are interchangeable.

Our Noisy Earth
Noise pollution is a threat to our well-being.
   I. Sources of noise pollution
      A. Vehicles
         1. Trucks
         2. Cars
         3. Buses
         4. Airplanes
         5. Motorcycles

II. Effects of noise pollution
   A. Loss of hearing
   B. Increase of tension
      1. Physical tension
      2. Mental tension
      3. Emotional tension
   C. Loss of energy
III. Solutions for noise pollution
   A. Stricter laws
   B. Better planning
   C. More citizen concern